simple handmade garden *furniture*

23 step-by-step weekend projects

Philip and Kate Haxell

LAUREL GLEN

San Diego, California

Contents

Introduction	**4**
Perfect Planters	**7**
Chunky Bamboo Planter	8
Auricula Plant Theater	11
Decorated Planter	16
Wall-Hanging Pot Holders	18
Hanging Basket Ladder	20
Relaxing in the Yard	**23**
Yard Chair	24
Checkers Table	31
Building Block Chair & Table	34
Barbecue Table	40
Love Seat	46

For Ann, Colin, Jackie, John, and Michael.

Laurel Glen Publishing
An imprint of the Advantage Publishers Group
5880 Oberlin Drive, San Diego, CA 92121-4794
www.advantagebooksonline.com

Copyright © Cico Books, 2001

Library-of-Congress Cataloging-in-Publication Data

Haxell, Philip.
  Simple handmade garden furniture:over 20 step-by-step weekend projects/ Philip and Kate Haxell.
     p. cm.
  ISBN 1-57145-720-8
     1. Outdoor furniture--Design and construction. 2. Garden ornaments and furniture--Design and construction. 3. Woodwork. I. Haxell, Kate. II. Title.

TT197.5.O9 H39 2002
684. 1'8--dc21
                                                    2001056855

Editor: Kate Haxell; Photographer: Lucinda Symons; Stylist: Denise Brock; Designer: Roger Daniels

1 2 3 4 5 06 05 04 03 02

Introduction

For so many of us our gardens are now an extension of our homes; we eat in them, work in them, play in them, relax in them—we also decorate them. Home improvement stores are now full of furniture and ornaments for the garden, and there is a wide range of weatherproof paints and stains available with which you can personalize your fences and benches.

Wanting to turn our own new garden into an outdoor room, we started looking at garden furniture. However, we were disappointed in the design and quality available at the cheaper end of the market, and horrified at the price we had to pay for items at the top end. We had already made furniture for inside our home and decided to do the same for our garden. Hence this book, which is full of interesting and original projects, some of which will enhance your own garden, whether it is a rustic country plot or an urban city yard.

There is a wide range of projects in this book, from very simple ones—perfect for beginners—to woodworking and more involved pieces. Some of the furniture projects have a lot of steps—but don't be intimidated. No project requires any special woodworking skills, just care and attention in cutting and fixing. Read the steps through carefully, and consult the comprehensive techniques section at the back of the book before you start a project. If you are unsure of a technique, simply practice it on an

extra piece of wood before embarking on the actual project.

You don't need a lot of expensive equipment to make these projects; take a look at the Toolbox on page 116, and just buy the tools you need to get started. As you progress, and hopefully become increasingly enthusiastic, you can invest in more equipment as you need it. It is a good idea to borrow or rent an expensive tool before you buy to make sure that you are happy using it. Always follow the safety instructions accompanying a tool carefully—taking risks or cutting corners can lead to trouble.

We have made suggestions for decorating the projects, but, of course, you can finish them to complement your own garden and planting schemes. Always use the best weatherproof paints and stains you can get, and remember that softwood furniture is not totally hardy. You should revarnish it each year, and store it indoors during the winter.

So get started, and soon you will be able to relax in your garden, enjoying the fruits of your labors.

PHILIP AND KATE HAXELL

Perfect Planters

Planters and decorative pots add character and depth to outdoor spaces. Decorate these practical, fragrant centerpieces to complement the flowers that you fill them with.

Chunky Bamboo Planter

Original and so simple to make, this planter will hold a range of small plants in a stylish display. Alternatively, plant herbs in it to make a miniature kitchen garden.

YOU WILL NEED

Thick bamboo
- 1 length: 39 in.
- 1 length: 32 in.
- 1 length: 24 in.
- 1 length: 16 in.
- 1 length: 8 in.

- Tape measure
- Crosscut saw
- Chisel
- Mallet
- Drill
- ⅛-in. drill bit

Thick copper wire
- 2 lengths: 24 in.
- 1 length: 20 in.
- 1 length: 16 in.
- 1 length: 12 in.

- Pin-nosed pliers

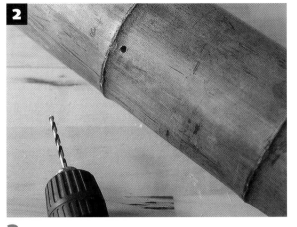

1 The internal membranes of the bamboo will hold soil for planting, but if a membrane is at the top of a length, you need to remove it to create enough depth. Use a chisel and mallet (see *Further Techniques*, page 112) to chip out the membrane.

2 Using a ⅛-in. drill bit (see *Core Techniques*, page 108), drill aligning holes in opposite sides of the 39-in. length of bamboo. The first pair of holes should be 2 in. up from the base, the second pair 4 in. further up, then a pair every 8 in. until you have five pairs of holes.

3 Drill holes in the 32-in. length of bamboo in the same way. Always working from the base up, continue to drill pairs of holes in the other lengths of bamboo. Obviously, as the lengths of bamboo get shorter, there will be fewer pairs of holes in each length.

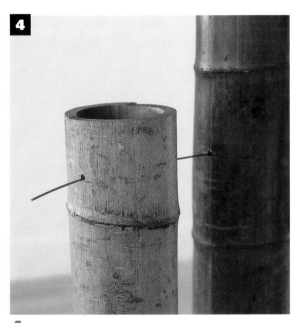

TIP

To feed the wire through the holes, position the bamboo with a light behind it. Look through the hole on one side, and feed the wire through the hole on the other side, then toward you and through the nearer hole. Wear safety goggles so that the wire doesn't poke you in the eye.

TIP

Using a pair of pin-nosed pliers, twist the ends of the wire into small curls for a stylish finishing touch.

4 Wire the lengths of bamboo together. Bend 2 inches of the other end of the 24-in. length of wire over at right angles, then thread one end through the lowest pair of aligning holes in the 39-in. length of bamboo.

Stand the 32-in. length of bamboo next to the 39-in. length, and thread the straight end of the wire through the lowest holes. Bend over one end of the second 24-in. length of wire, and thread it through the next pairs of holes up in both lengths of bamboo. Continue, using progressively shorter lengths of wire, until the two pieces are wired together through all the holes. Working from the bottom up, thread the wires through the holes in the 24-in. length of bamboo. Continue until all the pieces of bamboo are wired together. Push them up tightly against each other and bend over the free ends of the wire.

Auricula Plant Theater

Whether you stand it in a greenhouse or in the yard, this

planter provides the perfect auditorium for a colorful display.

Paint it to complement the flowers you choose.

YOU WILL NEED

Sides

Marine plywood

- 1 piece:
  ½ x 29½ x 31½ in.

Shelves

Marine plywood

- 1 piece:
  ½ x 26½ x 35 in.

Birch ply

- 1 piece:
  ⅛ x 4 x 37½ in.
- 1 piece:
  ⅛ x 4 x 31½ in.
- 1 piece:
  ⅛ x 4 x 19½ in.
- 1 piece:
  ⅛ x 2⅞ x 14½ in.

Quadrant

- 2 lengths:½ x 3 in.

Half-round dowel

- 2 lengths:
  ½ x 43¾ in.
- Shelf templates on
  page 118
- Jigsaw
- Tape measure
- Pencil
- Drill

- ³/₁₆-in. drill bit
- Countersink bit
- Wood glue

Screws

- 32: 1 in.

- Screwdriver
- Pinning gun
- ⅝-in. pins
- 120-grit sandpaper
- Sanding block
- Backsaw
- Masking tape
- Filler
- Primer
- Waterproof paint
- Paintbrush

1 Using a jigsaw (see *Core Techniques*, page 108), cut the side piece of plywood diagonally into two triangles.

2 On the 29¹/₂-in. side of both triangles, measure and mark vertical pencil lines at 4¹/₂ in., 11 in., and 18⁷/₈ in. from the 31¹/₂ in. side. Extend the pencil lines up to meet

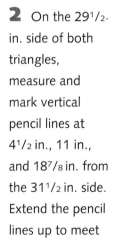

the sloping side. At the top of the longest line, cut a slot ¹/₈ x 2⁷/₈ in.; this can be achieved by jigsawing 2⁷/₈ in. down the line and then jigsawing down again, right next to the first line. On the next two lines, cut ¹/₈ x 4 in. slots in the same way.

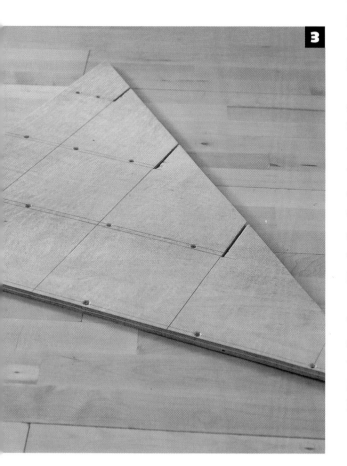

3 On both triangles, draw a horizontal line from the bottom of each slot, at right angles to the slot, extending across to the 31¹/₂-in. side of the triangle. Draw a parallel line ¼ in. above each horizontal line to give three pairs of parallel lines. The remainder of this step is worked on the upper line of only these pairs of lines.

On the line from the top slot, predrill and countersink (see *Core Techniques*, page 109) a ³/₁₆-in. hole 2 in. from each end. On the line from the middle slot, predrill and countersink three ³/₁₆-in. holes, with one hole 2 in. from each end, and one hole evenly spaced between them. On the line from the lowest slot, predrill and countersink four ³/₁₆-in. holes, with one hole 2 in. from each end and two holes evenly spaced between them.

Draw a line along the 29¹/₂-in. side of both triangles, ¼ in. up from the edge. Predrill and countersink five ³/₁₆-in. holes, with one hole 2 in. from each end and three more evenly spaced between them. Make sure that you countersink the holes on the outside face of each triangle.

4 Lay out the two triangles, countersunk-side down, with the two 31½-in. sides butted together. Working on these 31¹/₂-in. sides, and using a jigsaw, cut a ½-in.-wide strip off the triangle on the left. On the triangle on the right, draw two lines, parallel to and ¹/₄ in. and ½ in. in from the edge. On the ¹/₄ in. line, predrill and countersink five ³/₁₆ in. holes, with one hole 2¾ in. from each end and three more evenly spaced between them.

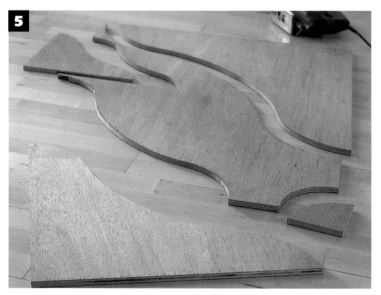

5 Enlarge the shelf templates by 400 percent and transfer them onto the marine plywood (see *Template Techniques*, page 114) in the arrangement shown above. Using a jigsaw, cut out the shapes.

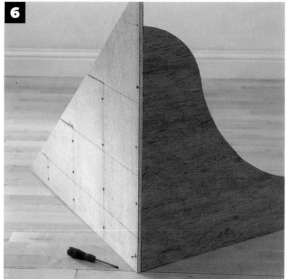

6 Glue and screw (see *Core Techniques*, page 109) the largest shelf to the bottom of the smaller triangle, aligning the back edge of the triangle with the corner of the shelf. Drive screws through the predrilled holes in the triangle into the edge of the shelf; do this carefully to avoid splitting the wood.

7 Stand the triangle up so that it rests on the shelf. Glue and screw the larger triangle to the smaller one, lapping the back edge of the larger triangle over the back edge of the smaller one. Drive screws through the predrilled holes in the larger triangle into the edge of the smaller one and into the edge of the bottom shelf.

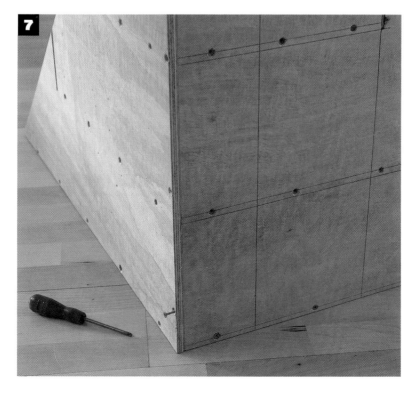

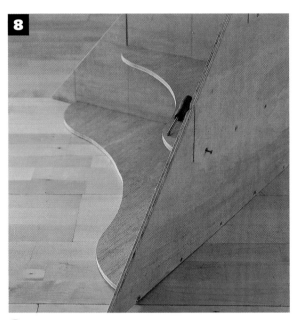

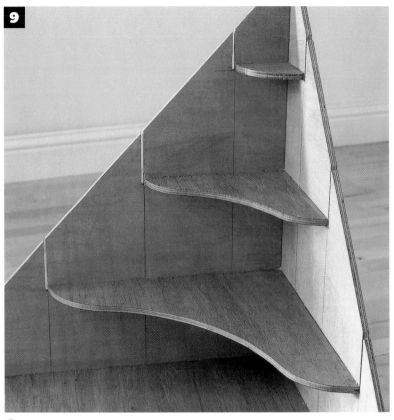

8 Glue and screw the second largest shelf in position above the bottom one. Align the shelf with the lower penciled line, and drive screws through the predrilled holes in the triangles into the edge of the shelf.

9 Glue and screw the remaining two shelves in position in the same way. The front edges of the top three shelves should all align with the relevant slots.

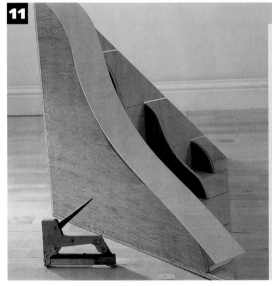

TIP

Leave the pieces of plywood to soak in cold water the night before you want to use them. They will be far more flexible when wet.

10 Glue and staple (see *Further Techniques*, page 112) a length of quadrant to each side of the bottom shelf, with one flat face aligned with the front edge of the shelf and the other against the side of the plant theater.

11 Glue and staple the longest piece of birch to the front edge of the bottom shelf. Start in the middle and work out to one side, then the other. At each end, glue and staple the birch to the length of quadrant.

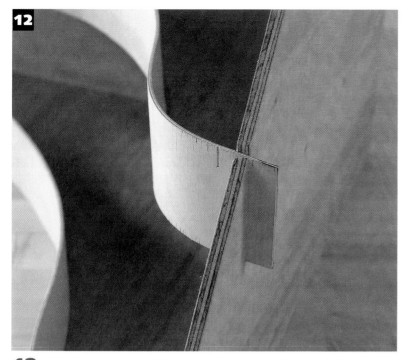

13 When the glue is dry (approximately 30 minutes), use a backsaw (see *Core Techniques*, page 108) to cut off the excess birch plywood sticking out of the slots.

12 Spread glue in the slots at each end of the next shelf up. Slide the ends of the second-longest piece of birch plywood into the slots. Gently press the middle of the plywood until it touches the edge of the shelf. Glue and staple the plywood to the front of the shelf as before. Staple the remaining two pieces of plywood to the upper shelves in the same way.

14 At the top of the triangle, one point sticks up above the other. Following the line of the lower side, sand (see *Finishing Techniques*, page 114) the protruding point down to make one smooth, central point.

15 Hold a length of half-round dowel in place along the front edge of a triangle. Mark a vertical line on the dowel at the top of the triangle, and using a backsaw, cut along it. Repeat on the other triangle. Glue both pieces on, using strips of masking tape to hold the dowel in place while the glue dries. Fill all the screw holes (see *Finishing Techniques*, page 112), sand the whole plant theater, and prime it, then paint it with two coats of waterproof paint.

Decorated Planter

Why not make your own planter to show off a display of herbs or your favorite plants? Simple to make, it can also be personalized easily by drilling a row of decorative holes or adding bands of mosaic tiles.

YOU WILL NEED

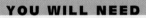

Trough

Pine board
- 2 pieces: ¾ x 10 x 24 in.
- 2 pieces: ¾ x 10 x 10 in.

Lumber
- 8 pieces: ¾ x 2 x 10 in.

Legs

Lumber
- 4 pieces: 1¾ x 1¾ x 36 in.

Rails

Lumber
- 2 pieces: ¾ x 1¾ x 24 in.
- 2 pieces: ¾ x 1¾ x 10 in.

- Drill
- ³/₁₆-in. drill bit
- Countersink bit
- Tape measure

Screws
- 40: 1⅝ in.

- Screwdriver
- Hammer

Nails
- 16: 1 in.

- Pencil
- ¾-in. spade bit
- Filler
- 120-grit sandpaper
- Sanding block
- Primer
- Waterproof paint
- Paintbrush

1 Predrill and countersink (see *Core Techniques*, page 109) four ³/₁₆-in. holes in the short sides of each piece of pine board. Position the holes ³/₈ in. from the edge, with one hole 1¹/₄ in. from each end and two more evenly spaced between them. Lap the long pieces of pine board over the edges of the short pieces, and glue and screw them together (see *Core Techniques*, page 109), driving screws through the predrilled holes into the edges of the short pieces.

2 Predrill and countersink two $^3/_{16}$-in. holes in each end of each side of the trough, $1^1/_4$ in. from the ends. On the long sides, position one hole $1^5/_8$ in. and one hole $8^1/_2$ in. from the top. On the short side, position one hole $1^1/_2$ in. and one hole $8^1/_4$ in. from the top. Spread glue over the top 8 in. of two sides of each leg. Place a leg in each corner of the trough, with the glued sides touching the trough and the top of the leg 1 in. below the top of the trough. Screw through the predrilled holes in the sides.

3 Place one of the eight trough slats against the legs, flush with the base of the trough, and hammer (see *Core Techniques*, page 109) a 1-in. nail through the sides into it. Nail another slat to the other end in the same way. Space the remaining six slats evenly along the trough, and nail them in place.

4 Predrill and countersink a $^3/_{16}$-in. hole in each end of each rail. Position the holes centrally $^3/_4$ in. from each end. Measure and mark 6 in. up from the bottom of each leg. Fasten a long rail between the legs, driving screws through the predrilled holes at the marked points. Fasten the short rails between the legs in the same way.

5 Measure and mark a line 2 in. down from the top edge, right around the trough. Starting $2^3/_8$ in. from each end and using a $^3/_4$-in. spade bit, drill (see *Further Techniques*, page 111) a row of evenly spaced holes along each side of the trough. Fill all screw holes, sand the planter, and prime, then paint it with two coats of waterproof paint (see *Finishing Techniques*, page 114).

TIP

Instead of drilling holes, you can create a summer look by decorating the planter with mosaic tiles. Paint the planter a soft green or blue before gluing tiles in contrasting colors along the top and bottom edges. Add more decorative strips of mosaic to contrast with new plantings or to add new colors to your yard.

Float flowers up your walls with these clever pot holders. They may seem unsupported, but they are in fact completely sturdy, as well as being simple to make.

Wall-Hanging Pot Holders

YOU WILL NEED

Lumber
- 1 piece: ¾ x 8¼ x 14¼ in.
- 1 piece: ⅜ x ¾ x 14¼ in.

- Template on page 119
- Jigsaw
- Drill
- ³⁄₁₆-in. and ¹⁄₁₆-in. drill bits
- Tape measure
- Pencil
- Backsaw
- Masking tape
- Countersink bit

Screws
- 2: ⅝ in.

- Screwdriver
- 120-grit sandpaper
- Sanding block
- Exterior wood stain
- Paintbrush

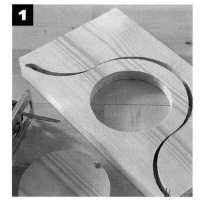

1 Enlarge the template by 133 percent and transfer it onto the large piece of lumber (see *Template Techniques*, page 114). Using a jigsaw and drill, cut out the inner hole first (see *Further Techniques*, page 110), then the outer shape.

2 Cut a rabbet along the back edge of the holder. Draw a line on the underside of the holder, 3/4 in. from the edge. Draw another line on the back edge, 3/8 in. from the base. Stick a length of masking tape to the blade of a backsaw, 3/8 in. from the cutting edge. Using a backsaw (see *Core Techniques*, page 108), saw along the line on the underside of the holder, making sure that you do not cut deeper than the tape.

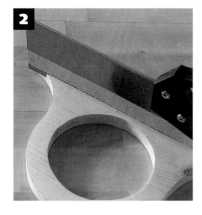

TIP

If you want to make more than one pot holder, screw two pieces of lumber together through the holes marked on the template before you do step 1, and cut out the two shapes together.

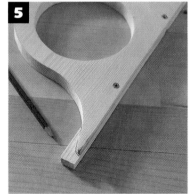

3 Remove the tape from the saw, and cut along the line on the back edge of the holder. The two saw lines must meet so that the rabbet is cut out. Discard.

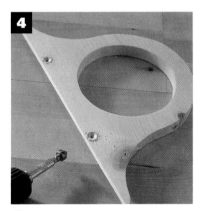

4 Predrill and countersink (see *Core Techniques*, page 109) two 3/16-in. holes in the holder, as marked on the template. Countersink on the side without the rabbet.

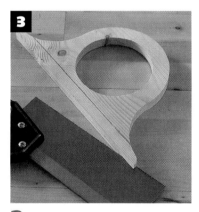

5 Fit the small piece of timber into the rabbet and drill two 1/16-in. pilot holes down through the predrilled holes in the holder into the timber. Drive a screw through each hole. Draw around the curve of the holder onto the piece of lumber in the rabbet.

6 Using a backsaw, cut away the excess wood outside the marked curves. Unscrew the piece of lumber, and predrill and countersink two 3/16-in. holes through it on the narrow edge, with one hole 2 3/4 in. from each end. The countersinking must be on the curved front. Screw the lumber back into the rabbet, and sand it to follow the curve. Stain the holder with exterior wood stain (see *Finishing Techniques*, page 114).

TIP

To hang the holder, screw through the holes in the rabbet lumber into the wall. Use wall plugs on a masonry wall. Fit the holder over the lumber, and screw through the predrilled holes.

Hanging Basket Ladder

Create extra space in your yard by making a ladder for hanging baskets and pots, which will show off your smaller plants and allow them to be moved easily in and out of the shade.

YOU WILL NEED

Dowel
- 2 lengths: 2⅜ x 63 in.
- 4 lengths: ¾ x 16 in.

- Exterior wood stain and varnish
- Paintbrush
- Tape measure
- Pencil
- Masking tape
- Drill
- ¾-in. spade bit
- ³⁄₁₆-in. drill bit
- Wood glue
- Mallet

Screws
- 8: 1¼ in.

- Screwdriver
- Filler
- 120-grit sandpaper
- Sanding block

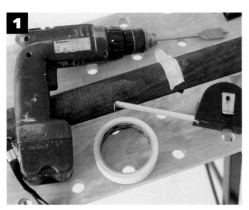

1 Paint the long poles with exterior wood stain (see *Finishing Techniques*, page 114). Measure 12, 24, 36, and 48 in. from one end of each long pole and mark the points by wrapping a piece of masking tape around each of the poles.

NOTE: This ladder is designed only as a plant holder; it is not for climbing.

2 Clamp the long dowels firmly, and using a ³/₄-in. spade bit, drill holes (see *Further Techniques*, page 111) for the treads through the masking tape; it is important that the holes are exactly in line with each other, or the ladder will be misshapen. The holes should not go right through the dowel, so wrap a piece of masking tape around the bit 1¹/₄ in. from the point, and drill until you reach the tape (see *Further Techniques*, page 110). Using a ³/₁₆-in. drill bit, drill from the bottom of each ³/₄-in. hole right through the dowel. Countersink (see *Core Techniques*, page 109) these holes on the outside of the dowels.

3 With one dowel still firmly clamped, spread a little glue (see *Core Techniques*, page 109) around one end of each of the short poles, and push them into the drilled holes. Spread glue around the other ends of the short poles, and fit the other long dowel on top of them. Use a mallet to knock the ladder together firmly.

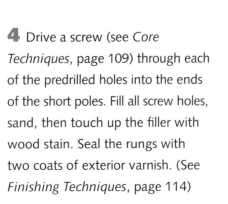

4 Drive a screw (see *Core Techniques*, page 109) through each of the predrilled holes into the ends of the short poles. Fill all screw holes, sand, then touch up the filler with wood stain. Seal the rungs with two coats of exterior varnish. (See *Finishing Techniques*, page 114)

Relaxing in the Yard

Elegant furniture will both enhance your whole yard and turn a sunny corner into a comfortable summer retreat.

Yard Chair

Stunning to look at and so comfortable to sit in, this chair is also deceptively easy to make. The legs are simply duplicated shapes, so follow the templates accurately, and it will all slot together.

YOU WILL NEED

Legs
Lumber
- 7 pieces: ¾ x 5½ x 37½ in.
- 2 pieces: ¾ x 5½ x 23¼ in.

Seat
Lumber
- 4 pieces: ¾ x 5¾ x 23¾ in.
- 2 pieces: ¾ x 1¾ x 15½ in.

Arms
Lumber
- 2 pieces: ¾ x 2¾ x 8¼ in.

Rails
Birch ply
- 2 pieces: ⅛ x 5½ x 45¼ in.
- 2 pieces: ⅛ x 5½ x 44½ in.

- Leg, seat, arm, and rail templates on page 120
- Jigsaw
- Pencil
- Backsaw
- ¾-in.-wide chisel
- Mallet
- 120-grit sandpaper
- Sanding block
- Drill
- ³⁄₁₆-in. and ¹⁄₁₆-in. bits
- Countersink bit
- Wood glue

Screws
- 14: 1¼ in.
- 2: 1½ in.
- 9: 2 in.

- Screwdriver
- Staple gun
- ⅝-in. staples
- Clamps
- Filler
- Exterior wood stain or varnish
- Paintbrush

1 Enlarge the full leg template by 500 percent, and transfer it onto five of the long pieces of leg lumber (see *Template Techniques*, page 114). Using a jigsaw (see *Core Techniques*, page 108), cut out five full legs. Cut out the notches marked on the template at either end of each leg and just one central notch, the one within the shaded area. To cut a notch, mark the lines on the wood in pencil, and using a backsaw (see *Core Techniques*, page 108), cut along these marked lines.

TIP
The lumber is too thick to screw the pieces together and cut out identical legs in the normal way. To speed up the process of cutting out the legs, you can cut the template out in thin MDF, and use a router with a template profiler bit to cut out the pieces (see *Template Techniques*, page 115).

2 Using a chisel and mallet (see *Further Techniques*, page 112), chisel out the wood between the two saw lines. Sand (see *Finishing Techniques*, page 113) the legs smooth, but do not sand into the notches.

3 Transfer the template onto the remaining two long pieces of leg lumber. Using a jigsaw, cut out two more full legs. Cut out the notches at either end and both of the central notches.

Cut down the full leg template to the shaded area to make the short leg template, and transfer it onto the two short pieces of leg lumber. Using a jigsaw, cut out two short legs with the two marked notches.

Predrill and countersink (see *Core Techniques*, page 109) 3/16-in. holes through all of the central notches on all legs, as marked. The countersinking must be on the unnotched side of each leg.

You will have a total of seven full legs—five with a single central notch and two with double central notches—and two short legs. Sand all the legs as before.

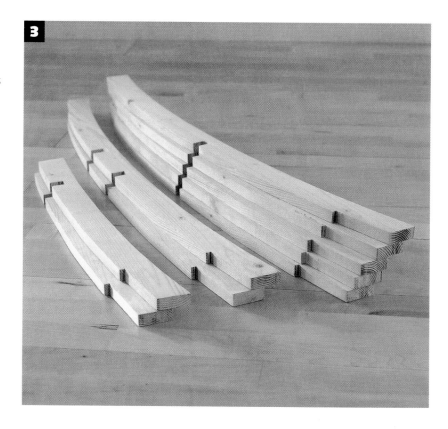

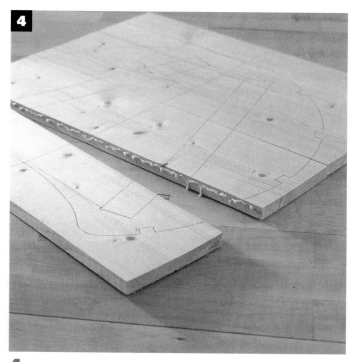

4 Lay the four large pieces of seat lumber side-by-side. Enlarge the seat template by 500 percent, and transfer it onto the lumber, including the marked batten positions (see *Template Techniques*, page 114). Glue the edges of the planks together (see *Core Techniques*, page 109), ensuring that the template aligns.

5 Predrill and countersink six 3/16-in. holes in the two seat battens, as marked on the template. Glue and screw (see *Core Techniques*, page 109) the battens to the seat, driving 1 1/4-in. screws through the predrilled holes. When the glue has dried, cut out the seat shape, notching the edges, as marked on the template, in the same way as the legs were notched. Sand the edges smooth, but do not sand into the notches.

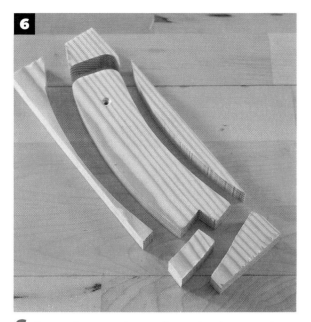

6 Screw the two pieces of arm lumber together (see *Template Techniques*, page 115). Enlarge the arm template by 500 percent, and transfer it onto the lumber. Using a jigsaw, cut out the arms as shown, and predrill and countersink a ³⁄₁₆-in. hole, as marked on the template. Sand the edges, and smooth and unscrew the pieces of lumber to give two identical shapes.

7 Enlarge the top rail template by 500 percent. Using a staple gun (see *Further Techniques*, page 112), staple the two shorter pieces of rail plywood together at either end, and transfer the template onto them, including the vertical lines. Using a jigsaw, cut out the shape as shown and then remove the staples. Enlarge the bottom rail template by 500 percent. Staple the two longer pieces of rail plywood together, and transfer the template onto them. Cut out the shape as before and remove the staples.

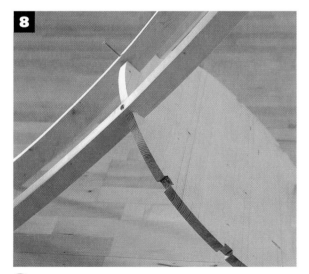

8 Lay out the five identical full legs, making sure that they are all right-side up. Working one at a time, spread some wood glue inside the central notches. Slide the notches in the legs into the five notches in the back of the seat—the central back notch and the two on either side of it. Drive a 2-in. screw through the predrilled hole in each leg into the edge of the seat.

9 Lay out the two identical full legs, again making sure that they are right-side up. Spread some wood glue inside the lower notch, and slide one into each of the next notches on either side of the seat. Drive a 2-in. screw through the predrilled hole in each leg into the edge of the seat.

10 Spread some wood glue inside the notch in the two short legs, and slide each one into the remaining notches on either side of the seat. Drive a 2-in. screw through the predrilled hole in each leg into the edge of the seat.

11 Fit the narrow end of each arm into the upper notch on the outer two full legs, and using a $^1/_{16}$-in. drill bit, drill a pilot hole through the predrilled hole in the leg into the arm. Remove the arm, spread some glue in the notch, and replace the arm, positioning the predrilled hole in the front of the arm centrally over the short leg. Drive a 1¼-in. screw through the predrilled and piloted hole in the leg and a 1½-in. screw down through the predrilled hole in the arm into the short leg.

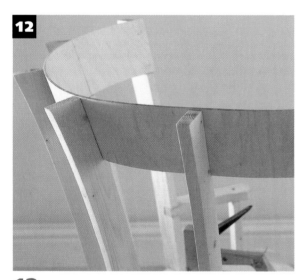

12 Spread some glue in the top notch of the center back leg. Take the top rail piece of plywood with the marked vertical lines, and position the middle line centrally in the notch. Using a staple gun and ⅝-in. staples, fire two staples through the wood, at the top and bottom, into the leg. Work around, gluing and stapling each vertical line on the wood to each leg in turn with two staples. On the two outer legs, use four evenly spaced staples to hold the wood firmly in position.

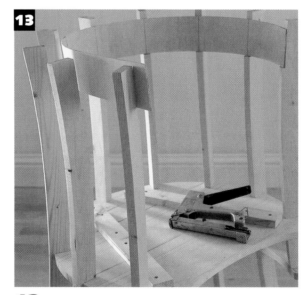

13 Turn the chair upside down, and staple on one of the bottom rail pieces in the same way.

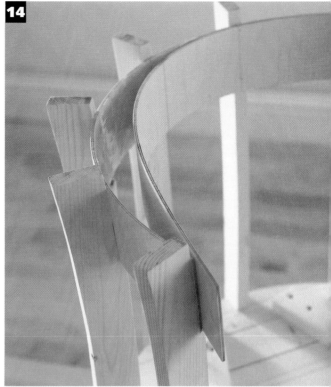

14 Spread wood glue over the inner surface of the bottom rail. Lay the second bottom-rail piece over the first one. Again starting in the middle, staple the rail to the legs, firing two pins through both layers of plywood into the lumber and four staples into each end leg.

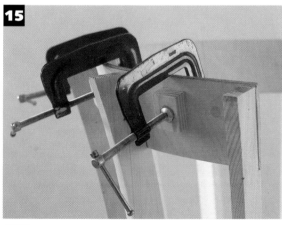

15 Clamp (see *Core Techniques*, page 109) the two layers of the rail together to hold the wood firmly in place while the glue dries—approximately 30 minutes. When this is dry, turn the chair right-side up, and glue and staple the second top-rail piece to the top rail in the same way as the bottom rail. Clamp it while it dries.

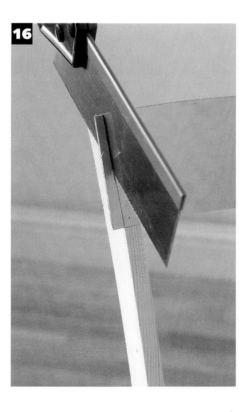

16 Using a backsaw, cut off any excess plywood where it protrudes beyond the final leg. Sand the chair thoroughly and fill all screw and staple holes, then paint the lumber with an exterior wood stain or varnish (see *Finishing Techniques*, page 114). This chair was painted with cherry-wood colored varnish.

Checkers Table

YOU WILL NEED

Frame

Lumber
- 2 pieces: ¾ x 2¾ x 15½ in.
- 2 pieces: ¾ x 2¾ x 17 in.
- 4 pieces: 1¾ x 1¾ x 17¾ in.

Top

Light wood-veneered MDF
- 1 piece: ½ x 19 x 19 in.

Lumber battens
- 4 pieces: ¾ x ¾ x 8¾ in.

Base

Marine plywood
- 1 piece: ¼ x 17 x 17 in.

- Drill
- ³/₁₆-in. drill bit
- Countersink bit
- Tape measure
- Pencil

Screws
- 16: 1½ in.
- 8: 1 in.

- Screwdriver
- Jigsaw
- Staple gun
- ⅝-in. staples
- Steel ruler
- Box cutter
- Square-ended, stiff artist's brush
- Colored varnish
- Filler
- 120-grit sandpaper
- Sanding block
- Clear gloss exterior varnish
- Paintbrush

Add an extra dimension to a drink table by checkering the top to turn it into a game table. The lid lifts off to store checkers and chess pieces or a book and sunglasses.

1 Predrill and countersink (see *Core Techniques*, page 109) two ³/₁₆-in. holes in each end of the narrow

pieces of frame lumber. Position one hole in a corner, ⅝ in. from the edges, and the other hole ⅝ in. up from the bottom edge and 1½ in. from the end, so that the two holes form a diagonal. Screw (see *Core Techniques*, page 109) one short piece to the ends of two square pieces of leg lumber, driving 1¹/₂-in. screws through the predrilled holes to make a half frame.

2 Screw one long piece of lumber to each side of a half frame, lapping the ends over the lumber of the half frame, as shown.

You will need to turn these long pieces of lumber upside down before screwing them on, so that the screws do not collide. Drive 1½-in. screws through the predrilled holes.

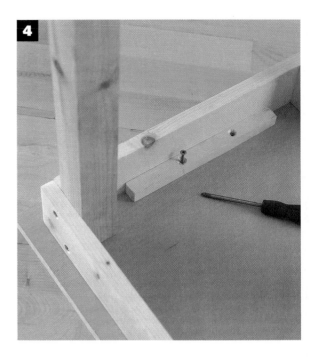

4 Place the frame, upside down, centrally on the square top piece. Predrill and countersink two ³⁄₁₆-in. holes in each top lumber batten. Position the holes centrally, with one 2¾ in. from each end.

Screw a batten to the top piece, butting it up to one side of the frame. Position the batten centrally along the frame and drive a 1-in. screw through the predrilled holes into the tabletop.

3 Slot the remaining half frame between the open ends of the long pieces of lumber, and screw in place, as before, to make a complete frame.

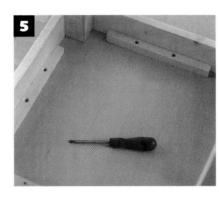

5 Screw the other three battens into place in the same way.

6 Measure and mark a 1³⁄₄-in. square within each corner of the plywood base. Using a jigsaw (see *Core Techniques*, page 108), cut out the squares.

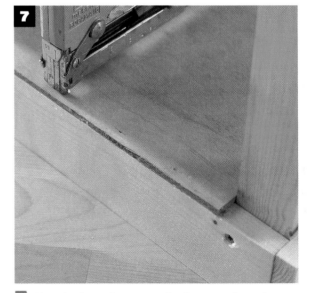

7 Slot the base between the legs, and staple (see *Further Techniques*, page 112) it to the bottom edge of the frame.

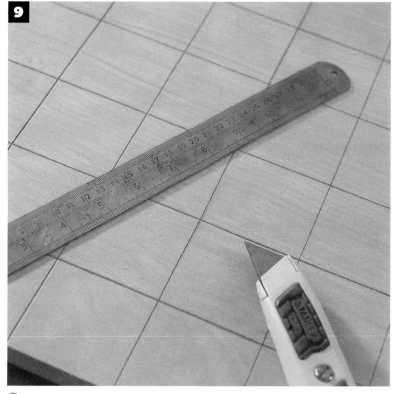

8 Using a pencil and steel ruler, divide the tabletop into 2³/₈-in. squares—eight across and eight down to make 64 squares.

9 With a box cutter and a steel ruler, cut lightly along the penciled lines; the cuts will help to keep the colored varnish from bleeding across into adjacent squares.

TIP

Make your own checkers pieces from slices of pole, sanded and painted with colored and clear varnish.

10 Using a square-ended, stiff artist's brush, paint alternate squares with colored varnish, being careful not to spread the varnish onto adjacent squares. When the colored varnish is dry, fill and sand all screw holes and then seal the whole table with two coats of clear gloss exterior varnish (see *Finishing Techniques*, page 114).

Building Block Chair & Table

Children will love this fun furniture designed especially for them that also provides useful storage for outdoor toys. Once you have built the cube, get them to help decorate it by painting on their favorite designs.

YOU WILL NEED

Sides

Marine plywood

- 2 pieces: ⅜ x 22¾ x 23⅝ in.

Base

Marine plywood

- 1 piece: ½ x 23⅝ x 23⅝ in.

Desk

Marine plywood

- 1 piece: ⅜ x 22¾ x 22⅞ in.
- 1 piece: ⅜ x 23⅝ x 23⅝ in.

Quadrant

- 2 lengths: ¾ x 22¾ in.
- 2 lengths: ¾ x 21¼ in.
- 2 lengths: ¾ x 19¾ in.
- 2 lengths: ¾ x 10¼ in.

Chair

Marine plywood

- 1 piece: ⅜ x 22¾ x 22⅞ in.
- 1 piece: ⅜ x 13 x 22⅞ in.

Quadrant

- 2 lengths: ¾ x 22¾ in.
- 2 lengths: ¾ x 21¼ in.
- 2 lengths: ¾ x 10½ in.
- 2 lengths: ¾ x 12 in.

- Side and base templates on page 121
- Jigsaw
- Drill
- ³⁄₁₆-in. drill bit
- Countersink bit
- Tape measure
- Pencil
- Wood glue

Screws

- 116: ¾ in.

- Screwdriver
- Filler
- 120-grit sandpaper
- Sanding block
- Primer
- Emulsion paints
- Paintbrush
- Sticky designs
- Waterproof varnish

1 Enlarge the side template by 500 percent, and transfer it onto each of the side pieces of plywood (see *Template Techniques*, page 114). Using a jigsaw (see *Core Techniques*, page 108), cut out the shapes. Predrill and countersink (see *Core Techniques*, page 109) ³/₁₆-in. holes, as marked on the template.

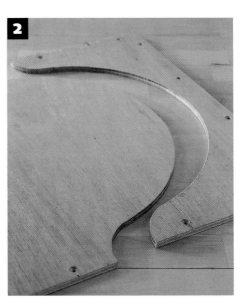

2 Enlarge the base template by 500 percent, and transfer it onto the base piece of plywood. Using a jigsaw, cut out the shapes. Predrill and countersink ³/₁₆-in. holes, as marked on the template.

3 Predrill and countersink ³/₁₆-in. holes on all four sides of the 22¾ x 22⅞-in. desk-back piece of plywood. Position the holes ¹/₄ in. in from the edges, with one hole 1⁵/₈ in. from each corner and two more evenly spaced between them. Glue and screw (see *Core Techniques*, page 109) a 22³/₄-in. length of quadrant to each of the 22³/₄-in. sides and a 21¹/₄-in. length to the other two sides, driving screws through the predrilled holes.

4 Glue and screw one of the larger side pieces to each of the 22³/₄-in. sides of the desk back. Drive screws through the predrilled holes in the plywood side pieces.

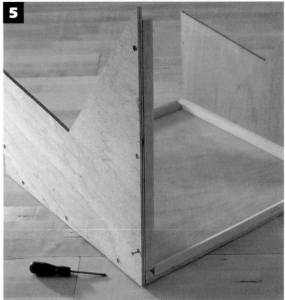

The building block also provides temporary storage for toys, though it will not keep them dry.

5 Glue and screw a 19³/₄-in. length of quadrant to each of the long edges of the sides, driving screws through the predrilled holes in the plywood.

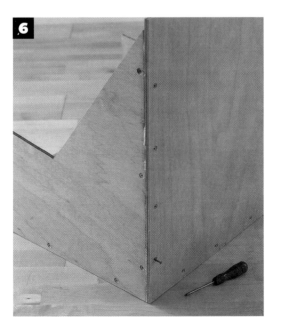

6 Predrill and countersink ³/₁₆-in. holes along three sides of the 23⁵/₈ x 23⁵/₈-in. desktop-piece of plywood. Position the holes ³/₄ in. in from the edges, with one hole 4³/₄ in. from each corner and two more evenly spaced between them. Screw the desktop to the sides and back of the desk, driving screws through the predrilled holes.

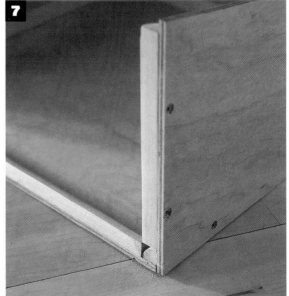

7 Glue and screw a 10¹/₄-in. length of quadrant to each of the short edges of the sides, driving screws through the predrilled holes in the plywood.

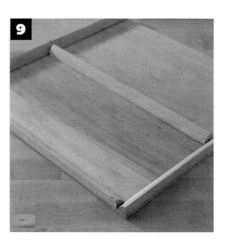

9 Predrill and countersink ³/₁₆-in. holes on two 22³/₄-in. sides and one 22⁷/₈-in. side (the base) of the 22¾ x 22⅞ in. chair-back piece of plywood. Position the holes ¹/₄ in. in from the edges, with one hole 1⁵/₈ in. from each corner and two more evenly spaced between them. Measure up 11 in. from the base, and mark a line across the wood. Predrill and countersink holes on this line. Position one hole 1⁵/₈ in. from each side with two more evenly spaced between them.

Using the method shown in step 3, glue and screw a 22¾-in. length of quadrant to each of the 22³/₄-in. sides and a 21¹/₄-in. length to the other side, driving screws through the predrilled holes in the plywood. Glue and screw the remaining length of 21¼-in. quadrant to the plywood, driving screws through the predrilled holes 11 in. up from the base.

8 Glue and screw the bottom section with the tongue to the sides and back of the desk, driving screws through the predrilled holes in the plywood.

10 Glue and screw one of the smaller side pieces to each of the 22³/₄-in. sides of the chair back. Drive screws through the predrilled holes in the plywood side pieces.

11 Glue and screw a 10¹/₂-in. length of quadrant to each of the short, straight edges of the sides and a 12-in. length of quadrant to the predrilled holes across the middle. Drive screws through the predrilled holes in the plywood side pieces.

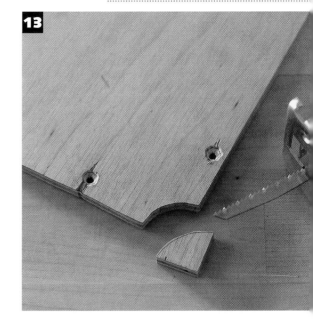

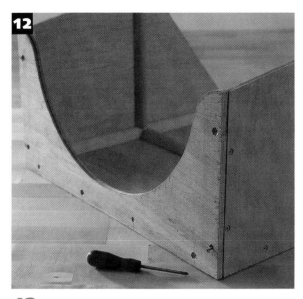

12 Glue and screw the remaining bottom piece to the sides and back of the chair, driving screws through the predrilled holes in the plywood.

13 Predrill and countersink ³/₁₆-in. holes on one long side and two short sides of the 13 x 22⅞ in. seat piece. On the long side, position the holes ⁵/₁₆ in. in from the edges, with one hole 2½ in. from each end and two more evenly spaced between them. On the short sides, position the holes at the same distances from the edge and ends, with one hole between them. Stand a cutoff piece of quadrant on the back corners of the seat and draw around it. Using a jigsaw, cut out the curved notch.

14 Glue and screw the seat to the quadrant that is positioned halfway up the chair, driving screws through the predrilled holes in the plywood.

15 Fill all screw holes and sand all the edges and corners to curves (see *Finishing Techniques*, page 114). On the top of the chair, sand the quadrant down to follow the slope (see inset). Prime and then paint the chair and table with emulsion paint (see *Finishing Techniques*, page 114). To add designs, fit the table and chair together to make a cube and apply the decoration. Either enlarge some favorite designs and paint them in emulsion paints, or get a local sign maker (look in a local telephone directory) to cut sticky vinyl shapes. Apply these to the cube, cutting them along the lines where the cube splits, and then seal the whole cube with two coats of waterproof varnish.

Barbecue Table

A perfect piece of furniture for patio cooks, this table has built-in storage space at each end to hold bottles of sauce, napkins, and cutlery, and a shelf underneath for plates and glasses. The top can be scrubbed down and has room for food preparation.

YOU WILL NEED

Top

Tongue-and-groove floorboards

- 4 pieces: ⅞ x 5 x 40½ in.

Lumber battens

- 3 pieces: ¾ x 1¾ x 14½ in.

Legs

Marine plywood

- 2 pieces: ½ x 9¼ x 17⅞ in.

Lumber

- 4 pieces: 1¾ x 1¾ x 31½ in.

Sides

Marine plywood

- 2 pieces: ½ x 9¼ x 48 in.

Storage spaces

Marine plywood

- 2 pieces: ½ x 4⅜ x 17⅞ in.
- 4 pieces: ½ x 4⅞ x 9⅛ in.

- 2 pieces: ⅛ x 5¾ x 19 in.

Shelf

Lumber

- 2 pieces: ¾ x 1¾ x 36⅝ in.

Marine plywood

- 1 piece: ½ x 14½ x 33⅛ in.

- Side and storage partition templates on page 122
- Jigsaw
- Wood glue
- Drill
- ³⁄₁₆-in. drill bit
- Countersink bit
- Tape measure
- Pencil

Screws

- 44: 1½ in.
- 8: 1¼ in.
- 12: ¾ in.

- Screwdriver
- Staple gun
- ⅝-in. staples
- Filler
- 120-grit sandpaper
- Sanding block
- Primer
- Satinwood paint
- Paintbrush
- Tung or Danish oil

1 Using a jigsaw (see *Core Techniques*, page 108), cut the groove off one of the floorboards.

2 Using a jigsaw, cut the tongue off another floorboard.

3 Glue (see *Core Techniques*, page 109) the four pieces of board together to make the table top. Fit the tongues into the grooves so that the outer edges are without tongues and grooves.

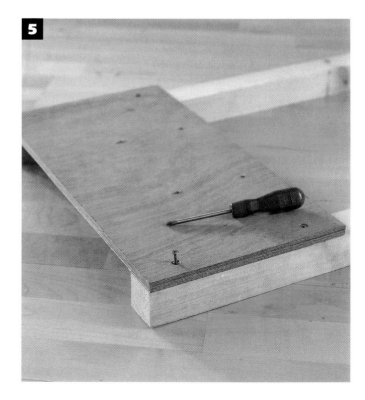

4 Predrill and countersink (see *Core Techniques*, page 109) six $^3/_{16}$-in. holes in each of the lumber battens. Position the holes $1^1/_2$ in., $2^7/_8$ in., $6^1/_2$ in., 8 in., $12^1/_8$ in., and $13^1/_4$ in. from one end. Glue and screw (see *Core Techniques*, page 109) the battens to the underside of the tabletop, driving $1^1/_2$-in. screws through the predrilled holes. Position the battens centrally across the four pieces of board, with one batten $1^7/_8$ in. from each end and the third one in the middle; the predrilled holes should sit at either side of the joints between the boards.

5 Predrill and countersink $^3/_{16}$-in. holes in both pieces of leg plywood. On one long (bottom) edge, position four holes $1^5/_8$ in. up from the edge, with two holes $^7/_8$ in. and two 6 in. in from each side. Position two more holes: one $5^1/_8$ in. up from the same long edge and one 6 in. in from each side. On the opposite long (top) edge, position three holes $^3/_8$ in. down from the edge, one hole $3^5/_8$ in. from each side, and one in the middle. On the same long edge, position two more holes $1^5/_8$ in. down from the edge and one $^7/_8$ in. in from each side.

Glue and screw one piece of leg lumber to each short side of each piece of plywood, aligning the ends of the lumber with the top edge of the plywood. Drive $1^1/_2$-in. screws through the two corresponding predrilled holes to make a pair of end legs.

TIP

The hanging shelves made for the potting shed (see page 62), are also wonderful for barbecues. Hang them near your cooking station and they will hold all your condiments and spices within easy reach.

6 Lay the tabletop face down, and fit one of the end legs over each of the outer battens on the underside. Glue and screw the end legs to the battens, driving 1½-in. screws through the three corresponding predrilled holes in the plywood.

7 Screw the two side pieces of plywood together (see *Template Techniques*, page 115). Enlarge the side template by 665 percent and transfer it onto the plywood (see *Template Techniques*, page 114). Using a jigsaw, cut out the two sides. Predrill and countersink ³⁄₁₆-in. holes, as marked on the template. Unscrew to make two identical shapes.

8 Glue and screw the sides to the leg lumbers, driving 1½-in. screws through the predrilled holes.

9 Predrill and countersink two ³/₁₆-in. holes in both 4⅜ x 17⅞-in. front pieces of plywood. Position the holes 1³/₄ in. down from one long (top) edge, with one hole 6 in. in from each side. Glue and screw the storage space fronts between the ends of the side pieces, driving 1¹/₄-in. screws through the predrilled holes in the sides into the edges of the front pieces.

10 Screw together two of the 4⅞-in. storage-space partition pieces of plywood. Cut the side template down to the shaded section to make the storage-partition template, and transfer it onto the plywood. Cut out two partitions. Unscrew to give two identical shapes. Repeat with the other two storage partition pieces.

11 Slide two partitions into each storage space, aligning each piece with the predrilled holes in the fronts and end legs, and making sure that the square ends of the partitions are flush with the base of the fronts and end legs. Drive ¾-in. screws through the predrilled holes into the edges of all of the partitions.

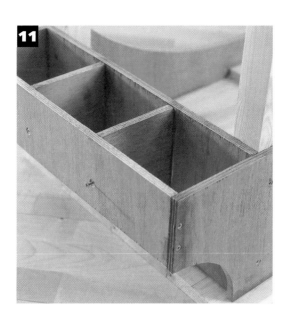

12 Staple (see *Further Techniques*, page 112) one 5¾ x 19-in. piece of plywood to the base of each of the storage spaces, firing the staples into the edges of the fronts, end legs, and partitions.

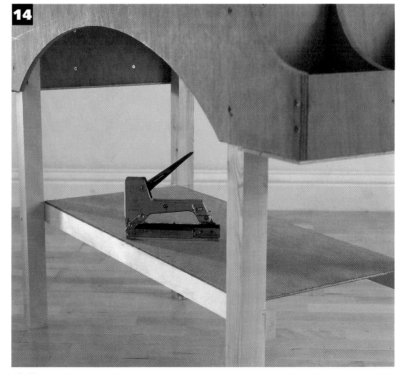

13 Predrill and countersink a ³/₁₆-in. hole 1 in. from each end of both lumber shelf pieces. Measure and mark 12 in. up from the base of each leg. Glue and screw the shelf lumbers between the legs at the marked points, driving 1¹/₂-in. screws through the predrilled holes into the legs.

14 Fit the shelf piece of plywood onto the rails and staple in place, firing staples into the rails. Fill all screw and staple holes, then sand all surfaces. Prime everything but the table top with acrylic primer, then paint it with satinwood paint (see *Finishing Techniques*, page 114). Oil the tabletop with tung oil or Danish oil.

Love Seat

This elegantly curving love seat proves that woodwork doesn't have to be

square. Don't be put off by the number of steps in this project; it really isn't

that complicated to make, and the end result is well worth the work.

YOU WILL NEED

Marine plywood
- 6 pieces: ¾ x 23 x 31½ in.

Lumber
- 2 pieces: 2 x ¾ x 29½ in.

Dowel
- 4 lengths: 1⅜ x 29½ in.

Birch ply
- 2 pieces: ⅛ x 11¾ x 96 in.
- 2 pieces: ⅛ x ¾ x 96 in.

- Seat and rail templates on page 122
- Jigsaw
- 120-grit sandpaper
- Sanding block
- Drill
- ³⁄₁₆-in. drill bit
- Countersink bit
- Tape measure
- Pencil
- 1-in.-wide chisel
- Mallet
- 1⅜-in. hole saw
- Backsaw
- Wood glue

Screws
- 21: 2 in.
- 30: 1¼ in.

- Screwdriver
- Staple gun
- ⅝-in. staples
- Paintbrush
- Water
- Box cutter
- Filler
- Primer
- Waterproof paint

1 Screw two pieces of marine plywood together (see *Template Techniques*, page 115). Enlarge the seat template by 400 percent and transfer it onto the wood (see *Template Techniques*, page 114). Using a jigsaw (see *Core Techniques*, page 108), cut out the seat shape and sand the edges smooth (see *Finishing Techniques*, page 113). Unscrew to make two identical shapes. Set one seat aside.

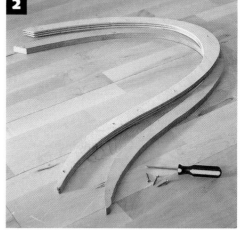

2 Cut the seat template down to the shaded section to make the rail template. Screw two of the remaining pieces of marine plywood together. Transfer the rail template onto the wood, and using a jigsaw, cut out the rail shapes and sand the edges smooth. Unscrew to make two identical shapes. Repeat with the two remaining pieces of plywood, then set these rails aside.

3 Predrill and countersink (see *Core Techniques*, page 109) three ³⁄₁₆-in. holes in one piece of lumber and two pieces of dowel. Position the first hole 2¹⁄₈ in. from one end, the next 18 in. from the same end, and the third hole ³⁄₈ in. from the other end.

Using a chisel and mallet (see *Further Techniques*, page 112), cut three ³⁄₄ x ³⁄₄-in. notches in the piece of lumber, each one centered over a drilled hole, as shown. At the end with the hole ³⁄₈ in. from it, the notch will make an L-shape in the end of the lumber.

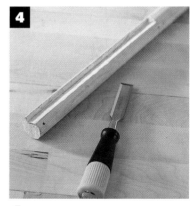

4 Take one piece of dowel and clamp it to the workbench, with the hole that is ³⁄₈ in. from an end nearest you, countersunk facedown. Starting at this end, draw, then chisel out (see *Further Techniques*, page 112) a groove ⁵⁄₈ in. wide, ¹⁄₈ in. deep, and 12 in. long to the left of the screw hole.

5 Using a 1³/₈-in. hole saw (see *Further Techniques*, page 111), cut a hole in the center back of two rails and the seat, as marked on the template.

6 Using a backsaw (see *Core Techniques*, page 108), cut away one side of the drilled hole on both rails and the seat, as shown.

7 Using a 1³/₈-in. hole saw, cut a crescent at one end of both rails and the seat, as marked on the template.

8 Lay one of the rails flat on the workbench; this will be the top of the chair. Take the dowel that you have not cut a groove in, and spread glue (see *Core Techniques*, page 109) around the end with the hole ³/₈ in. away from it.

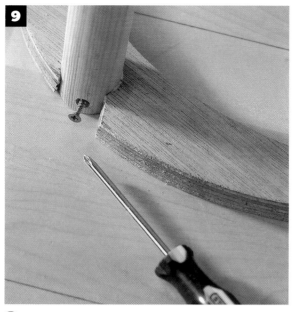

9 Slot this length of dowel into the center back hole in the rail, with the predrilled hole facing outward. Drive a 2-in. screw (see *Core Techniques*, page 109) through the predrilled hole into the plywood rail.

10 Spread glue around the predrilled end of the grooved piece of dowel. Slot this into the crescent-shaped hole, with one edge of the groove aligned with the outer edge of the rail, as shown. Drive in a 2-in. screw, as before.

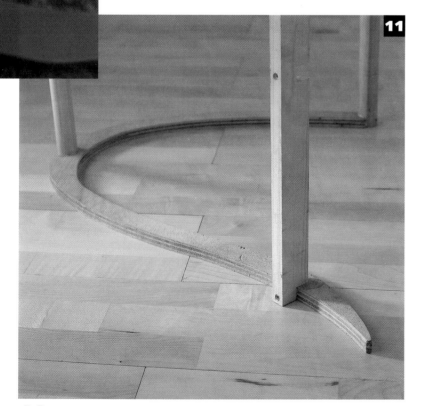

11 Screw the predrilled end of the notched piece of lumber to the other side of the rail with a 2-in. screw. Do not glue this, as it is a temporary strut to support the project firmly while it is being assembled.

12 Slot the seat over the legs, and push it down carefully until the edge of the seat fits into the central notch in the lumber and the predrilled holes align with the center of the edge of the seat. Ease the seat up a little, spread some glue on the dowels, and push the seat back down into position. Drive 2-in. screws through the dowels and the notched lumber into the seat, as before.

13 Slot the second rail over the legs, fitting it into the notch in the lumber and aligning it with the predrilled holes. Glue and screw, as before. Unscrew the length of notched lumber, and move it to the inside of the curve. Screw it in place, then lay the seat down with the grooved dowel flat on the floor.

14 Spread glue along the outer edges of the upper rail and seat, and along the inside of the groove in the dowel. Fit the short edge of one end of a piece of birch plywood into the groove and staple it (see *Further Techniques*, page 112) in place along this edge. Get someone to help you, as it can be tricky to handle the plywood by yourself.

15 Bend the plywood over the glued edges of the rail and the seat, stapling it in place as you go. The edges of the plywood should align with the outer edges of the rail and seat. Place the staples approximately 1¼ in. apart, though on the tighter parts of the curve they may need to be more frequent. Staple the plywood right around to the far end of the rail and seat, leaving the loose end free.

16 Glue and staple a narrow piece of birch plywood around the bottom rail in the same way.

Making the second seat

Make the second seat in exactly the same way, following steps 3–16 and using the remaining seat, rails, dowels, lumber, and birch plywood.

17 Stand the chairs upside down and facing in opposite directions. Unscrew and remove the notched lumber. Dilute some glue with water—one part glue to three parts water—and, using a paintbrush, paint it over the plywood on the outside of both chairs all the way to the ends of the loose flaps. Push the chairs up against one another so that the curves fit tightly together. Bend each flap around the back of the chair next to it, so that the glued side touches it, pressing it in place along the edges as you go.

18 Paint some diluted glue between the plywood bottom rails—where they touch—then bend each narrow piece around the bottom rail next to it, gluing and pressing them in the same way.

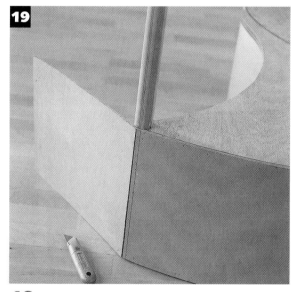

19 Cut off any excess plywood with a box cutter to score down the edges of the pieces at the points where they meet the legs and arms of the chairs. Score down several times until you have cut right through.

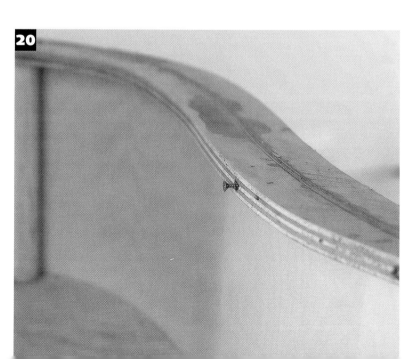

20 Predrill two $^3/_{16}$-in. holes through the top and bottom rails and the seat, as marked on the template. Drive in 2-in. screws.

Fill all screw and staple holes, the notches you cut in step 6, and the cut ends of the plywood. Sand the whole love seat, then prime and paint it with two coats of waterproof paint (see *Finishing Techniques*, page 114).

The Potting Shed

Every yard needs storage for tools and flowerpots, but there is no reason why it shouldn't be attractive, as well as practical.

Tool Rack

Adapt a traditional Shaker-style peg rail to make this tool rack. The shelf above provides storage and a peg for the tool caddy (see page 58) that will hold your small tools, and it hangs neatly next to your taller tools.

1 Screw the three large pieces of bracket lumber together (see *Template Techniques*, page 115). Enlarge the template by 400 percent, and transfer it onto the lumber (see *Template Techniques*, page 114). Using a jigsaw (see *Core Techniques*, page 108), cut out the bracket supports. Unscrew to make three identical shapes.

2 Predrill and countersink (see *Core Techniques*, page 109) three ³⁄₁₆-in. holes in the three long pieces of bracket lumber. Mark the center line and position one hole on the line 1¹⁄₂ in., one hole 4³⁄₈ in., and one hole 12 in. from the top. Glue and screw (see *Core Techniques*, page 109) one piece to the back of each bracket support, driving a 1¹⁄₂-in. screw through the top hole and a 1-in. screw through the middle hole.

YOU WILL NEED

Brackets
Lumber
- 3 pieces: ³⁄₄ x 5³⁄₄ x 8 in.
- 3 pieces: ³⁄₄ x 1³⁄₄ x 16¹⁄₂ in.
- 3 pieces: ³⁄₄ x 1³⁄₄ x 6³⁄₄ in.

Shelf
Lumber
- 3 pieces: ³⁄₄ x 1³⁄₄ x 57 in.
Spacers
- 2: ³⁄₄ in.

Peg rail
Lumber
- 1 piece: ³⁄₄ x 2³⁄₄ x 57 in.
Dowel
- 8 lengths: 1 x 5¹⁄₂ in.

- Template on page 123
- Jigsaw
- Drill
- ³⁄₁₆-in. drill bit
- Countersink bit
- Tape measure
- Pencil
- Wood glue
Screws
- 6: 1¹⁄₄ in.
- 18: 1¹⁄₂ in.

- Screwdriver
- 1-in. spade bit
- Mallet
- Try square
- Filler
- Sanding block
- 120-grit sandpaper
- Exterior wood stain
- Paintbrush

3 Predrill and countersink two ³⁄₁₆-in. holes in the three short pieces of bracket lumber. Mark the center line down each piece and position one hole on the line ³⁄₈ in. and one hole 4¹⁄₂ in. from the top. Glue and screw one piece to the top of each of the bracket supports, driving a 1¹⁄₂-in. screw through the first hole and a 1¹⁄₄-in. screw through the second hole.

4 Predrill ³⁄₁₆-in. holes in the three shelf rails. Mark the center line down each piece and position one hole on the line 4 in. from each end and one in the middle. Lay the brackets on their backs and align them with the predrilled holes in one of the shelf pieces. Drive a 1¹⁄₂-in. screw through each of the predrilled holes into the top of each bracket.

5 Place a ³⁄₄-in. spacer on each end of the rail, and lay another rail on its side on top of the first one. Drive in screws as before.

6 Remove the spacers and use them to position the third rail. Drive in screws as before.

7 Using a 1-in. spade bit (see *Further Techniques*, page 111), drill eight holes through the peg rail piece of lumber. Mark the center line down the piece and position one hole 4 in. from each end and the remaining six holes 7 in. apart. **NOTE:** These measurements give the position of the center of each hole.

8 Run a little glue (see *Core Techniques*, page 109) around one end of each length of dowel, and hammer it into a hole with a mallet. Use a try square to check that the dowels are at true right angles to the backboard.

9 Lay the peg rail peg-side down on the floor and position the brackets and shelf above it, with the ends of the brackets protruding 2⁵/₈ in. below the peg rail. Drive a 1½-in. screw through each of the predrilled holes in the bracket into the backboard. Fill all screw holes and sand the tool rack, then paint it with exterior wood stain (see *Finishing Techniques*, page 114).

Tool Caddy

YOU WILL NEED

Lumber

- 2 pieces: ¾ x 8¼ x 8¼ in.
- 3 pieces: ¾ x 4⅛ x 14⅛ in.
- 2 pieces: ¾ x 4⅛ x 6¼ in.

Dowel

- 1 length: 1 x 17½ in.

Plywood

- 1 piece: ⅛ x 7½ x 15¼ in.

- Template on page 123
- Jigsaw
- Drill
- 1-in. spade bit
- ³⁄₁₆-in. drill bit
- Countersink bit
- Tape measure
- Pencil
- Back saw
- ¾-in.-wide chisel
- Mallet
- Wood glue

Screws

- 8: 1⅝ in.

- Screwdriver
- Staple gun
- ⅝-in. staples
- Damp cloth
- Filler
- 120-grit sandpaper
- Sanding block
- Exterior wood stain
- Paintbrush

This is an excellent little piece of equipment that will hold all your small tools and paraphernalia as you work around the yard. As well as hanging on the tool rack (see page 55), it also fits on the end of the potting bench (see page 67).

1 Screw the two square pieces of lumber together (see *Template Techniques*, page 115). Enlarge the template by 400 percent and transfer it onto the lumber (see *Template Techniques*, page 114). Using a jigsaw (see *Core Techniques*, page 108), cut out the end pieces and drill the hole, as marked on the template, with a 1-in. spade bit (see *Further Techniques*, page 111). Predrill and countersink (see *Core Techniques*, page 109) ³⁄₁₆-in. holes, as marked on the template. Unscrew to make two identical shapes.

2 On one long piece of lumber, measure and mark pencil lines 2³/₁₆-in. long. Position one line 4¹/₄ in. from either end and a second, parallel line 5 in. from either end. Using a backsaw (see *Core Techniques*, page 108), saw along the marked lines.

3 Chisel out the wood (see *Further Techniques*, page 112) between the saw lines to make two ³/₄ x 2³/₁₆-in. slots. Saw and chisel an identical slot in the middle of each of the two short pieces of lumber.

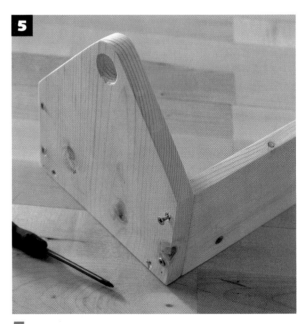

4 Slot the short pieces into the long piece, as shown, to make the tool container dividers.

5 Glue and screw (see *Core Techniques*, page 109) one long side piece to an end piece, driving screws through the predrilled holes in the end piece.

6 Position the dividers against the end and side pieces. Glue and screw the second side piece to the end piece, as before, making sure that it is tight against the dividers.

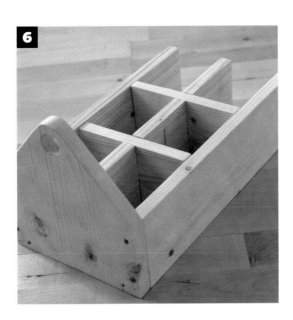

7 Screw the other end piece in place, driving screws through the predrilled holes in the end.

8 Staple (see *Further Techniques*, page 112) the piece of plywood to the base of the container. Staple through the plywood into the sides and ends.

9 Thread the length of dowel through the drilled holes in the ends of the container. Position the dowel centrally, then pull it back slightly and spread a little glue around it (see *Core Techniques*, page 109). Push the dowel back into place. Wipe away any excess glue with a damp cloth. Fill all screw holes and sand the container, then paint it with exterior wood stain (see *Finishing Techniques*, page 114).

Hanging Shelves

These shelves are the simplest project in this book, and

yet they are so useful. Hang them inside or outside the

potting shed to store pots and dishes, or to display

plants. Hung next to the barbecue table (see page 43),

they will hold tools and condiments for creative cooking.

1 Round off the corners of the pieces of lumber with sandpaper and chamfer the edges (see *Finishing Techniques*, page 114). Drill (see *Core Techniques*, page 108) a 1/4-in. hole in each corner of each piece of lumber. The holes in the two back corners are 3/4 in. from each edge; the holes in the two front corners are 3/4 in. from the front edge and 1 in. from the side edge.

YOU WILL NEED

Timber
• 3 pieces: 3/4 x 5½ x 19½ in.
Dowel
• 1 length: 1½ x 19½ in.
Cord
• 2 lengths: ¼ x 78 in.

• 120-grit sandpaper
• Sanding block
• Tape measure
• Pencil
• Drill
• ¼-in. and 3/16-in. drill bits
• Countersink bit
• Masking tape
• Backsaw
• ½-in.-wide chisel
• Mallet
• Exterior wood stain
• Paintbrush

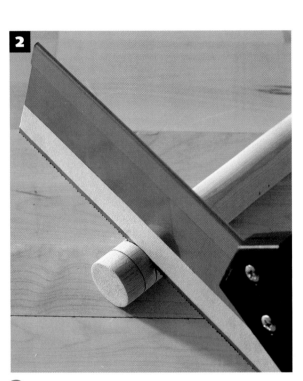

3 Using a chisel and mallet (see *Further Techniques*, page 112), chisel out the wood between the saw lines to make a $^1/_2$-in.-wide trench, $^1/_4$ in. deep. Stain all the pieces of lumber and the length of dowel with exterior wood stain.

2 Predrill and countersink (see *Core Techniques*, page 109) two $^3/_{16}$-in. holes in the length of dowel, with one hole 3$^1/_8$ in. from each end. Mark a pencil line around the dowel $^5/_8$ in. from each end and a second pencil line 1$^1/_8$ in. from each end. Put a piece of tape along the blade of a backsaw, $^1/_4$ in. up from the cutting edge, and saw (see *Core Techniques*, page 108) around all the pencil lines, ensuring that you do not cut deeper than the tape.

4 Tie a knot in one end of each length of cord, and put tape around the other end to keep it from fraying. Thread the taped end of each length through one of the back holes in a piece of lumber, and pull it through up to the knot.

5 Measure up the cords 8 in. from the top of the shelf and make pencil marks. Tie knots in the cords so that the pencil marks sit exactly at the top of the knots. Thread the lengths of cord through the back holes in the second shelf. Measure, knot the cords, and thread them through the top shelf in the same way. The spacing between the knots must be accurate or the finished shelves will not hang straight.

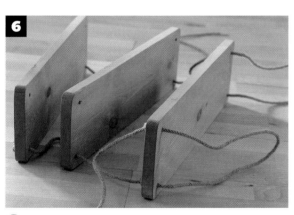

6 Measure up the cords 24 in. from the top of the top shelf and make pencil marks. Thread the cords down through the front holes in the top shelf and then tie knots so that the pencil marks sit exactly at the top of the knots. Thread the cords down through the front holes in the other two shelves, knotting them below each one; adjust the knots until the shelves are level.

7 Loop each 24 in. of cord around the trench in each end of the dowel. At the back of the shelves, the cord runs around the outer edge of the trench, moving to the inner edge at the front.

To hang the shelves, drive appropriate screws through the predrilled holes in the dowel into the wall you want to hang them from. If you are hanging the shelves from a masonry wall, use wall plugs.

Potting Bench

This well-designed bench is easy to make. The top lifts off, so once your bedding plants are ready to be planted, you can carry the top, with all the plants, to your garden.

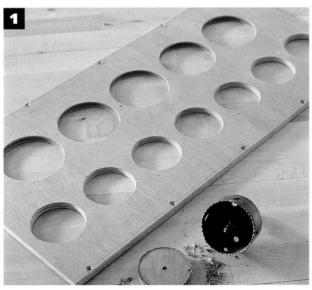

1 Using hole saws (see *Further Techniques*, page 111), cut out five 4-in. and seven 3⅛-in. holes in the large top piece to make the bench top. (These sized holes will accommodate standard flower pots, but you can drill any sized holes, in any arrangement.) Predrill and countersink (see *Core Techniques*, page 109) five ³⁄₁₆-in. holes along both long sides. Position the holes ¼ in. in from the edge, with one hole 1¼ in. from each end and three more evenly spaced between them.

YOU WILL NEED

Top
Marine plywood
- 1 piece: ½ x 13¾ x 28¼ in.
- 2 pieces: ½ x 4 x 28¼ in.

Legs and frame
Marine plywood
- 2 pieces: ½ x 12¾ x 32¼ in.
- 2 pieces: ½ x 11 x 32¼ in.
- 2 pieces: ½ x 6½ x 13¾ in.

Dowel
- 2 lengths: ¾ x 51½ in.
- 2 lengths: ¾ x 42¾ in.
- 16 lengths: ¼ x 1⅝ in.

- End leg, side leg, and top leg templates on page 123
- Drill
- 4-in. and 3⅛-in. hole saws
- ³⁄₁₆-in. and ¹⁄₄-in. drill bits
- Countersink bit
- Tape measure
- Pencil
- Wood glue

Screws
- 44: 1¼ in.
- 4: 1½ in.

- Screwdriver
- Jigsaw
- ¾-in. spade bit
- Damp cloth
- Filler
- 120-grit sandpaper
- Sanding block
- Primer
- Waterproof paint
- Paintbrush

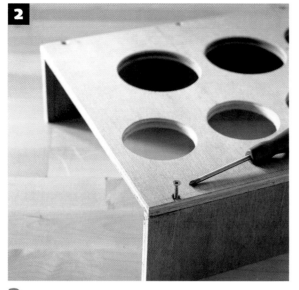

2 Glue and screw (see *Core Techniques*, page 109) the two long top pieces to the long sides of the top. Carefully drive 1¼-in. screws through the predrilled holes in the bench top into the edges of the sides.

3 Screw the two largest pieces of leg plywood together (see *Template Techniques*, page 115). Enlarge the end leg template by 400 percent and transfer it onto the plywood (see *Template Techniques*, page 114). Using a jigsaw (see *Core Techniques*, page 108), cut out the end legs. Using a ³/₄-in. spade bit (see *Further Techniques*, page 111), drill the four holes, as marked. Unscrew to make two identical shapes.

4 Screw the two second-largest pieces of leg plywood together. Cut the end leg template down to the shaded section to make the side leg template, and transfer it once onto the plywood. Using a jigsaw, cut out one pair of side legs, then turn the template around, transfer it onto the plywood again, and cut out the other pair of side legs, as shown. Predrill and countersink on both sides five ³/₁₆-in. holes along the long straight side. Position the holes ¼ in. in from the edge, with one hole 2 in. from the top, another 1¹/₄ in. from the bottom, and three more evenly spaced between them. Unscrew to make four identical shapes.

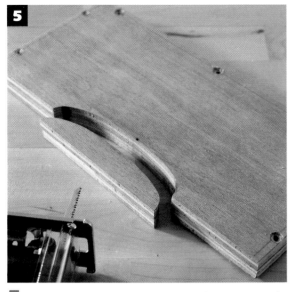

5 Screw the two smallest pieces of leg plywood together. Enlarge the leg top template by 400 percent and transfer it onto the plywood. Using a jigsaw, cut out the leg tops. Predrill and countersink $3/16$-in. holes along both short sides and the long straight side of the leg tops. Position the holes $1/4$ in. in from the edges, with one hole $1\frac{1}{4}$ in. from each corner on the short sides, and on the long straight side, one hole $2^3/8$ in. from each corner and another in the middle. Unscrew to make two identical shapes.

6 Glue and screw one side leg to each edge of an end leg. Drive $1^1/4$-in. screws through the predrilled holes in the side legs into the edge of the end leg; do this carefully to avoid splitting the plywood.

7 Glue and screw the leg top to the top of the assembled leg. Drive $1^1/4$-in. screws through the predrilled holes in the leg top into the edges of the end leg and side legs, as before. Make the other leg in the same way.

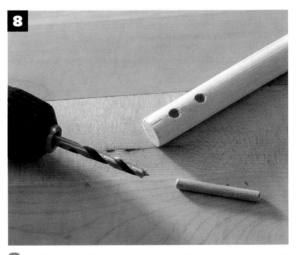

8 Drill $1/4$-in. holes through both long lengths of dowel to receive the $1/4$-in. dowel pegs. Position one hole $4^7/8$ in. from each end and a second hole $5^1/2$ in. from each end. Drill similar holes in both short lengths of dowel, positioning them $11/16$ in. and $1^1/2$ in. from each end.

9 Stand the legs upside down on the floor and lay the bench top upside down between them, leaving a gap of ³/₈ in. between the ends of the top and the legs. Thread a long length of dowel through corresponding holes in the tops of the end legs. Turn the dowel so that the holes in it are at right angles to the floor, and ensure that one hole is on each side of the end leg. Mark the position with a light pencil mark, then pull the dowel back slightly. Spread a little wood glue around the areas that will be inside the plywood and push the dowel back in. Wipe away any excess glue with a damp cloth.

10 Spread a little wood glue around the middle of a peg and push it through the drilled hole in the dowel. Wipe away any excess glue with a damp cloth. Spread glue on one end of another peg and push it into the hole on the inside of the leg (see inset). Thread and peg the other long length of dowel through the other pair of top holes in the same way.

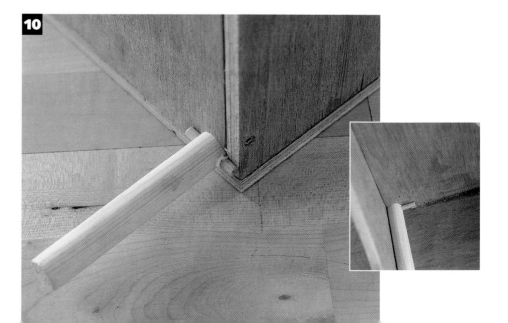

11 Thread and peg the two short lengths of dowel through the holes in the other ends of the legs in the same way.

12 Predrill and countersink a $3/16$-in. hole down through the leg tops into the dowels. Position one hole on each side of each leg top, 1 in. from the edge. Drive a $1^1/_2$-in. screw down through each hole. Fill all screw holes and sand the potting bench, then paint it with acrylic primer and two coats of waterproof paint (see *Finishing Techniques*, page 114).

A Rustic Retreat

Whether you live deep in the

country or in the heart of a city,

bring a touch of rural charm to

your yard with these traditionally

styled projects.

Picket Bench

This New-England–style bench, easily made from slats of timber, will find a home in the smallest yard. Paint it in a soft color to complement your summer planting scheme.

YOU WILL NEED

Back

Lumber
- 9 pieces: ¾ x 2¾ x 51 in.
- 3 pieces: ¾ x 1¾ x 37¼ in.

Spacers
- 1: ¾ x 2¾ x 2¾ in.
- 1: ¾ x 1¾ in.
- 1: ¾ x 2¾ x 11½ in.

Front

Lumber
- 9 pieces: ¾ x 2¾ x 17¾ in.
- 2 pieces: ¾ x 1¾ x 37¼ in.

Seat

Lumber
- 3 pieces: ¾ x 1¾ x 14¼ in.
- 4 pieces: ¾ x 2¾ x 37¼ in.

Spacers
- 3: ¾ x 1¾ in.

Braces
- 4 pieces: ¾ x 1¾ x 15½ in.
- 2 pieces: ¾ x 2¾ x 19½ in.

- Tape measure
- Pencil
- Jigsaw
- Drill
- ³⁄₁₆-in. drill bit
- Countersink bit

Screws
- 101: 1¼ in.

- Screwdriver
- Clamps
- Filler
- 120-grit sandpaper
- Sanding block
- Primer
- Waterproof paint
- Paintbrush

1 Measure down 1⁵⁄₈ in. on each side of one end of each of the nine pieces of back lumber. Draw a diagonal line from each measured point to the top center. Using a jigsaw (see *Core Techniques*, page 108), cut along the lines to make a pointed picket.

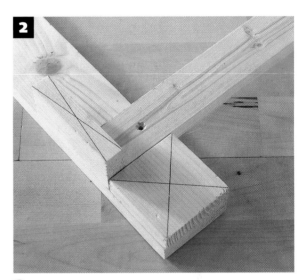

2 Predrill and countersink (see *Core Techniques*, page 109) nine ³⁄₁₆-in. holes in each of the the three back rails. Position the holes centrally, with one hole 1¹⁄₂ in. from each end, one hole 5 in. from each end, and the remaining five holes every 4¹⁄₂ in.

Lay the first picket flat, with the square spacer aligned with the square end. Lay one rail on the picket with the small spacer, lying on its ³⁄₄-in. side, aligned with both the side of the picket and the end of the rail. Drive a screw (see *Core Techniques*, page 109) through the predrilled hole. Remove all of the spacers.

TIP
Draw an X on the surface of each of the spacers so that you do not confuse them with the pieces of lumber needed to make the bench.

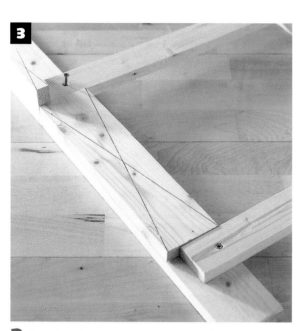

3 Position the long spacer above the rail. Lay the second rail above this, with the small spacer aligned with both the side of the picket and the end of the rail, as before. Drive a screw through the predrilled hole.

4 Use the small spacer, lying on its 1³/4-in. side, to set the width between the first and second pickets. Use the square and the long spacers, as before, to set the picket in the right position on the rails. Screw the picket in place. Continue until all nine pickets are screwed to the two rails.

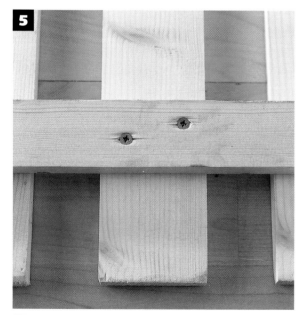

5 On the second and seventh pickets, drive another screw into each rail, at an angle to the first one, to keep the pickets from twisting on the rails.

6 Turn the bench back over and align the long spacer with the top of a picket point. Lay the third rail below it and screw it to each of the pickets in turn. Drive in an extra screw on the second and seventh pickets, as before.

7 Make the front of the bench in the same way as the back, using the same measurements. Use the square spacer to establish the position of the bottom rail and align the top rail with the top of the slats.

8 Make up the slatted bench seat using the same principles. Predrill and countersink four $^3/_{16}$-in. holes in the three rails. Position the holes centrally with one hole $1^1/_2$ in. and one hole $5^1/_2$ in. from each end. Lay the slats out, using the $1^3/_4$-in. side of a spacer to set the distance between them.

Lay one rail across the ends of the slats, using the $^3/_4$-in. side of the spacers to set the distances between one end of the rail and the side of the slats, and the side of the rail and end of the slats, as shown. This side of the seat will be the back of the bench. At the front, the other end of the rail will stop $1^1/_2$ in. from the side of the last slat. Screw the rail to the slats, driving screws through the predrilled holes.

9 Fix a rail across the other end of the slats in the same way, then measure the distance between the two rails and fix another rail centrally. Predrill and countersink five $^3/_{16}$-in. holes in each of the two outer slats. On the back slat, position the holes $^3/_8$ in. in from the edge, with one 4 in. from each end and three more evenly spaced between them. On the front slat, drill the holes the same distances apart, but position them $1^1/_8$ in. from the edge.

10 Lay the bench back down with the side with two rails uppermost. Position the seat so that the back slat sits over the higher of the two rails. Drive screws through the predrilled holes in the seat into the rail.

11 Stand the bench upright, and position the front under the front edge of the seat. Clamp in place. Drive screws through the predrilled holes in the seat into the front.

12 Predrill and countersink two $3/16$-in. holes in each end of each short brace piece. Position one hole $3/8$ in. from each corner. Glue and screw two braces across each end of the bench, as shown. Align the braces with the ends of the rails and drive screws through the predrilled holes into the end grain of the rails.

13 On the long braces, measure along 2 in. on one side, and draw a diagonal line across to the opposite corner. At the other end, measure and mark a parallel line. Using a jigsaw, cut along the lines.

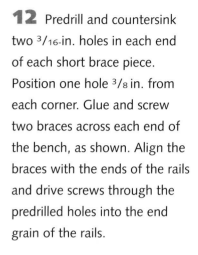

14 Glue and screw one diagonal brace across each end of the bench, behind the horizontal braces, so that they run in opposite directions at each end. Fill any screw holes and sand the bench, then prime and paint it with two coats of waterproof paint (see *Finishing Techniques*, page 114).

YOU WILL NEED

Tabletop

Lumber

- 6 pieces: ¾ x 3¾ x 37¾ in.

Battens

Lumber

- 2 pieces: 2 x 4 x19 in.
- 2 pieces: 2 x 4 x 10¼ in.

- Ceramic pot with 15¾-in.- diameter rim
- Wood glue
- Hammer
- Nail
- String
- Pencil
- Tape measure
- Miter block
- Backsaw
- Drill
- ³⁄₁₆-in. drill bit

Screws

- 32: 1 in.

- Screwdriver
- Jigsaw
- 120-grit sandpaper
- Sanding block
- Primer
- Waterproof paint
- Paintbrush

Herb Table

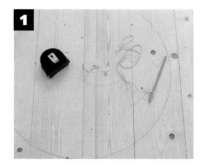

Make the most of your favorite corner of the yard with a tabletop that sits on top of a large pot. The central hole, through which the plants can grow, creates a living piece of furniture that will change with the passing seasons.

1 Butt up and glue (see *Core Techniques*, page 109) the six pieces of lumber to hold them while you mark the circles. Hammer a nail into the center of the lumbers, and tie one end of a length of string to it. Tie a pencil to the string 17³/₄ in. from the nail, and draw a circle for the outside of the tabletop. Draw an inner circle the diameter of your pot—in this case 15³/₄ in.

2 Miter the ends (see *Further Techniques*, page 110) of the battens across the 4-in. faces. Lay them within the two circles as shown, so that they cover as many of the lumbers as possible. Drill (see *Core Techniques*, page 109) ³/₁₆-in. holes and drive two screws through the battens into each piece of lumber.

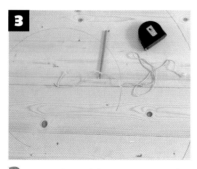

3 Turn the tabletop over and again mark two circles. Mark the same outer edge of 17³/₄ in. and a smaller inner circle of 14³/₄ in. for the central hole. This allows the tabletop to rest on the pot.

4 Using a drill and jigsaw, cut out the inner circle (see *Further Techniques*, page 110).

5 Using a jigsaw (see *Core Techniques*, page 108), cut around the outer circle. Sand the tabletop, then prime and paint it with two coats of waterproof paint (see *Finishing Techniques*, page 114).

Seat for a Child's Swing

Based on the design of a traditional spoke-back chair, this sturdy swing seat is far more pleasing to the eye than its plastic counterparts.

YOU WILL NEED

Seat

Plywood
- 1 piece:
  ½ x 12 x 21½ in.

Lumber
- 1 piece:
  ¾ x 9¾ x 21½ in.
- 1 piece:
  ¾ x 2 x 21½ in.

Rail

Lumber
- 2 pieces:
  ¾ x 9¾ x 21½ in.

Dowel
- 8 lengths: 1 x 8 in.
- Seat and rail templates on page 124
- Drill
- ³⁄₁₆-in. drill bit
- Countersink bit

- Jigsaw
- 120-grit sandpaper
- Sanding block
- ½-in. and 1-in. spade bits
- Wood glue
- Mallet

Screws
- 11: 1 in.
- 12: 1¼ in.

- Screwdriver
- Exterior varnish
- 2 lengths: ¾-in.-wide plastic-coated steel chain cut to length for installation

NOTE: This seat is not suitable for children under the age of three. Children must be supervised at all times while using the seat. Consult the Guidelines produced by the U.S. Consumer Product Safety Commission, Washington, D.C. 20207 before installation, toll-free telephone: 1-800-638-2772, or visit the CPSC website at www.cpsc.gov.

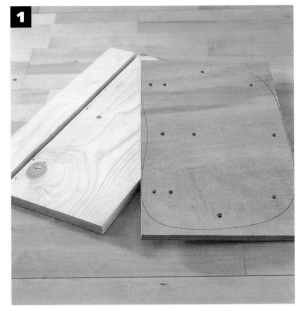

1 Enlarge the seat template by 400 percent and transfer it onto the seat plywood (see *Template Techniques*, page 114). Predrill and countersink (see *Core Techniques*, page 109) the eleven ³/₁₆-in. holes marked on the template with circles. Ensure that the two pieces of seat lumber are, when butted together, the same size as the piece of plywood.

2 Butt up the two pieces of lumber and screw them to the plywood (see *Core Techniques*, page 109), driving 1-in. screws through the predrilled holes. Cut out the seat shape with a jigsaw. Sand the edges smooth (see *Finishing Techniques*, page 114).

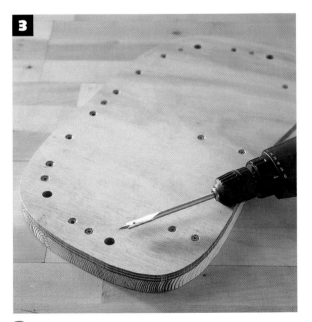

3 Predrill the eight ³/₁₆-in. holes marked on the template with crosses and the four ³/₄-in. holes marked with stars. Drill through both layers of wood. Unscrew the lumber and plywood, and countersink the newly drilled ³/₁₆-in. holes on the bottom of the plywood.

4 Drill 1-in. holes (see *Further Techniques*, page 111) in the lumber only, using the ³/₁₆-in. holes drilled in the last step as the center points. Position the point of the 1-in. spade bit in the ³/₁₆-in. hole and drill right through. Check that the holes will receive the pieces of 1-in. dowel, and sand the insides of the holes a little (see *Finishing Techniques*, page 114) if they are too tight.

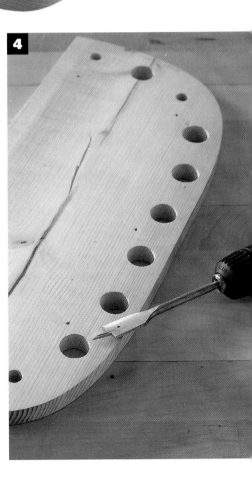

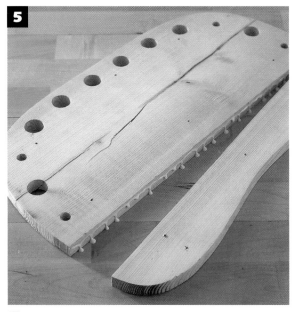

5 Glue the two pieces of lumber together. Glue and screw (see *Core Techniques*, page 109) the lumber to the plywood, driving 1-in. screws through the holes used in step 2.

6 Cut the seat template down to the shaded area to make the rail template, and transfer it onto the two pieces of rail lumber. Cut out the rails separately; if you screw the pieces of lumber together and then try and cut them, you will find that the thickness of the wood makes cutting the curve difficult. In one of the rails, redrill the five $^3/_{16}$-in. holes marked on the template with circles.

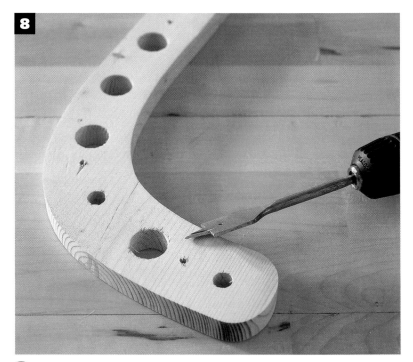

7 Screw the rails together, driving 1¼-in. screws through the predrilled holes. Sand the edges so that they are identical. Turn the arms over and drill the four $^3/_4$-in. holes marked on the template with stars. Drill right through both layers of lumber. Unscrew the rails.

8 Drill the eight 1-in. holes, marked on the template with crosses, in the rail in which you predrilled the holes in step 6. Check that the holes will receive the pieces of 1-in. dowel, and sand the insides a little if they are too tight. Glue and screw the rails back together, driving 1¼-in. screws through the holes used in step 7.

9 Spread a little glue around one end of each length of dowel, and push them into the 1-in. holes in the seat. Hammer them home with a mallet if necessary. Use a try square to check that they are at right angles.

10 Spread a little glue around the free end of each dowel and push the rail down onto them, so that one piece of dowel is located in each 1-in. hole in the underside of the rail. Tap the rail down with a mallet if necessary.

11 Turn the swing upside down and drive a 1¹/₄-in. screw through the predrilled holes in the plywood into each piece of dowel.

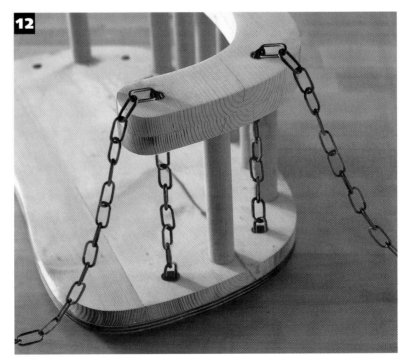

12 Paint the swing with two coats of exterior varnish (see *Finishing Techniques*, page 114). Thread a length of chain, cut to fit your chosen method of installation, down through the front hole in one side of the rail. Take it through the front hole in the seat, up through the back hole in the seat, and through the back hole in the rail. Repeat on the other side with the other piece of chain.

Japanese Arbor

Create a shady retreat in the sunniest of yards with this classical arbor. Although this is a substantial project, it is not difficult to construct, but you will need help when setting it up.

YOU WILL NEED

Roof

Rough-sawed, pressure-treated lumber

- 4 pieces: 1¾ x 4 x 59 in.
- 4 pieces: ¾ x 1¾ x 52½ in.
- 4 pieces: ¾ x 1¾ x 25¼ in.
- 4 pieces: ¾ x 1¾ x 6½ in.

Marine plywood

- 1 piece: ¾ x 43 x 78 in.

Split bamboo fencing

- 1 length: 70 x 195 in.
- 4 single strips: 70 in.

Posts

Rough-sawed, pressure-treated lumber

- 4 pieces: 3 x 3 x 70 in.

- End beam and roof support templates on page 124
- Jigsaw
- Drill
- ⅜ in. and ³⁄₁₆ in. drill bits
- Tape measure
- Try square
- Miter block
- Backsaw

Screws

- 20: 1½ in.
- 8: 1½ in.
- 4: 2 in.

- Screwdriver
- Combined wood stain and preservative
- Paintbrush
- Marker pen
- Small pruning shears
- Staple gun
- ⅜-in. staples

Fence-post holders

- 3 x 3 in.

- Sledgehammer
- Spirit level

Coach bolts with nuts and washers

- 4: ⅜ x 5½ in.

- ⅜-in. spanner

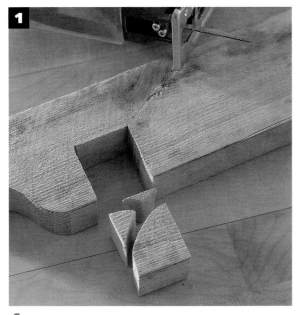

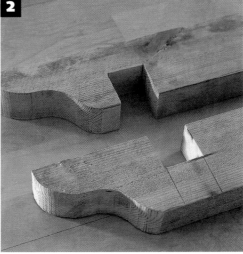

2 On the other two pieces of roof lumber, follow the unshaded area to cut out the housings. Two of the rails will have housings on the curled (bottom) side and two will have housings on the flat (top) side.

1 Enlarge the end beam template by 665 percent, and transfer it onto each end of the four longest pieces of roof lumber (see *Template Techniques*, page 114). Using a jigsaw (see *Core Techniques*, page 108), cut out the curled ends.

Using a jigsaw, cut out the shaded housings marked on the template on two of the pieces of lumber. Cut the two vertical slots first, then cut a curve from the outer end of the left-hand slot to the inner end of the right-hand slot, and remove the chunk of lumber. Cut another curve from as high as possible on the right-hand side to the inner end of the left-hand side, and remove the chunk of lumber. Finally, cut across the bottom of the housing and remove the last chunk of lumber.

3 Drill (see *Core Techniques*, page 108) a ⅜-in. hole through the center of each lumber post, 1⅝ in. from one end. Lay the drilled end of the post against one of the rails that has the housing cut from the top. Lay the top of the post 1 in. below the edge of the rail and butt it up to the side of the housing.

Use a try square to check that the angle between the post and the rail is ninety degrees. Drill down through the drilled hole in the post and right through the rail. Repeat at the other end of the rail with another post, and at both ends of the other rail with the housing, cut from the top.

4 Enlarge the roof-support template by 665 percent twice. Flip one over and tape the two together to make a symmetrical template. Transfer this twice onto the piece of plywood. If you lay the templates on the wood in the arrangement shown, they will take up a minimum of lumber. Using a jigsaw, cut out the roof supports. Cut out the housings marked on the template at the ends of the supports using the method described in step 1. Cut out the housings marked on the template in the center, so that one comes down from the top and the other goes from the bottom. Use the same method, but you will need to make more cuts, as these housings are deeper than the others.

5 Lay out the rails so that those with the drilled holes have the housing facing up. Lay the other two between them so that the housings slot into each other to form a square. It is important that this is a true square, so check by measuring the diagonals; they should be the same.

TIP
From this step on, it is best to make the arbor outside, as it is quite large and may not fit through a door once it has been put together.

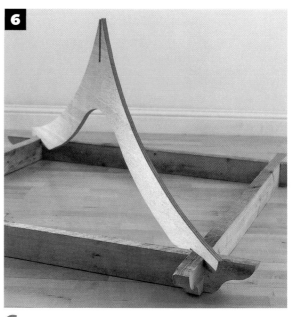

6 Take the roof support with the housing coming down from the top. Slot the housings in the ends across the square joints in the frames.

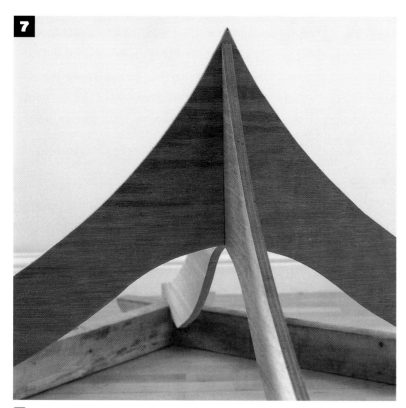

7 Slot the other roof support into the central housing in the first roof support, slotting the end housings across the square joints, as before.

8 Miter (see *Further Techniques*, page 110) each end of the four second-longest pieces of roof lumber across the 1¾-in. width. Predrill a ³/₁₆-in. hole in each end, at right angles to the miter. Position one hole 1 in. from the point at one end and one 2 in. from the point at the other end.

9 Lay the mitered pieces between the ends of the roof supports, one on each side and alternating the drilled ends so that the screws do not collide. Drive 1¹/₂-in. screws (see *Core Techniques*, page 109) through the holes 1 in. from the end and 2-in. screws through the holes 2 in. from the end.

10 Miter and predrill each end of the four next-longest pieces of roof lumber, but across the ¾-in. width. At one end, position the hole ⁵/₈ in. from the point and ⁵/₈ in. down the mitered face; at the other end, ⁵/₈ in. from the point and 1¹/₂ in. down the mitered face.

11 Lay a piece between the roof supports, moving it up until it fits across the width. Stagger the holes, as before, and drive a 1¹/₂-in. screw through each predrilled hole.

12 Miter each end of the shortest pieces of roof lumber and drill holes, as in step 10. Fit them between the roof supports and screw in place, as in step 11.

13 Lift the whole rooftop off the square frame and paint it with a combined wood stain and preservative (see *Finishing Techniques*, page 114).

14 Cut the split bamboo fencing into four lengths, each 47 in. long. Remove two single strips of bamboo from one end of each length, leaving the binding wire protruding; this will be the bottom edge.

Lay one length over one side of the roof, with two strips hanging over the rail at the bottom. Make sure that one of the binding wires runs up the center of the length of bamboo, so that once the bamboo is cut to size, this wire will hold the smallest lengths in place. Using a marker pen, roughly draw the outline of the roof onto the bamboo; draw the outlines approximately 1¹/₄ in. larger around. Using small pruning shears, cut out the outlines (do not use your best shears, as this will blunt them).

When cutting the bamboo to size, leave 4 in. of the binding wire protruding from the edge; these ends will be used to tie the lengths of bamboo together along the edges of the roof.

Lay a cut section against one side of the roof, and put in two or three staples to hold it in position. Fold the last two lengths of bamboo under, and align the edge of them with the edge of the lumber rail. Push the binding wire tails up between the pieces of bamboo, and wrap them around the binding wires to hold the fold in place.

15 Staple the bamboo to the lumber frame, stapling across the binding wires and through the pieces of bamboo into all of the pieces of roof lumber.

16 Using small pruning shears, trim the bamboo so that the edge aligns with the center of the roof support. Do not cut the binding wires—leave them protruding.

17 Lay one length of bamboo over the remaining three sides of the roof in turn. Fold, staple, and cut them in the same way.

18 Lay a single piece of bamboo over the corner joint between two trimmed edges. Twist the free lengths of wire together tightly over the piece of bamboo to hold it in place. Repeat on the remaining three corners.

TIP
To avoid buckling the edges of the post holders, lay a piece of flat wood over the top of them and hammer onto that.

19 Choose a completely flat piece of ground in your garden to set up the arbor. Lay out the roof beams in a square, as in step 5, in exactly the right spot. Using a sledgehammer, hammer a fence-post holder into the ground, tight to each corner, as shown. Hammer them down until only the square section shows above the ground. Remove the beams.

20 Push the posts into the post holders, making sure that the drilled holes in the tops all face front to back. The posts should go right down to the bottom of the holders; you may have to hammer them in with the sledgehammer. Using a spirit level, check that they are truly upright.

22 Slot the remaining two beams into the housings, as in step 5, to make a square frame. Using a spirit level, check that the beams are completely horizontal.

23 Lift the roof onto the frame, slotting the housings in the ends of the roof supports across the square joints in the frame, as in step 7. In each corner, drive a $1^5/8$-in. screw down through the lowest roof beam into the rail that it is resting on.

21 Bolt the beams with the housings cut from the top between the outside of two opposite pairs of posts. Push the bolts through the holes drilled in step 3, and use washers and nuts to fasten them tightly.

Willow Screen

Extremely simple to make, this screen will provide welcome shade

and protection from the wind. Alternatively, use it to hide an

unattractive compost bin or an untidy corner of the yard.

1 Predrill and countersink (see *Core Techniques*, page 109) four 1/4-in. holes in the long pieces of lumber. Position the holes centrally with one hole 7/8 in. from one end and one hole 6³/4 in. from the other end. Lay out the four pieces of lumber with the two short pieces between the longer pieces, level with the holes. Drive a 4-in. screw through each of the predrilled holes into the ends of the short pieces of lumber. Use a try square to check that the corners are 90°.

2 Miter (see *Further Techniques*, page 110) the ends of the two short lengths of D-section lumber. Predrill and countersink five ³/16-in. holes, with one hole 1¹/2 in. from each end and three more evenly spaced between them. Position the three middle holes centrally and the two end ones toward one edge to keep clear of the miter. Miter, predrill, and countersink the two long lengths of D-section lumber in the same way, spacing six holes evenly between the two end ones. Paint all lumber with colored exterior varnish; we used medium oak.

3 Lay the length of willow fencing over the lumber frame. The willow should lap over the width of the lumber by approximately two-thirds all around.

TIP

The easiest way to erect your screen is to use fencing posts, as with the Japanese arbor, page 82. Hammer them into the ground and slot the legs of the screen into them.

YOU WILL NEED

Lumber

- 2 pieces: 1¾ x 1¾ x 65 in.
- 2 pieces: 1¾ x 1¾ x 27¾ in.

Willow fencing

- 1 length: 26¾ x 58 in.

D-section timber

- 2 lengths: 2 x 31¼ in.
- 2 lengths: 2 x 59 in.

- Tape measure
- Pencil
- Drill
- ¼-in. and 4³⁄₁₆-in. bits

Screws

- 4: ¼ x 4 in.
- 26: 1¼ in.

- Screwdriver
- Miter block
- Backsaw
- Exterior varnish

Fence post holders

- 2: 1¾ x 1¾ in.

4 Lay a short length of D-section over the willow, across the bottom of the frame, aligning the lower edges of the lumber and D-section. Drive 1¼-in. screws through the predrilled holes into the lumber. Drive the screws through the D-section first, then adjust the willow so that the screws are going down between two branches.

5 Lay a long length of D-section along one side of the frame, ensuring that the mitered corner fits neatly into the miter on the short length, and screw in place, as before. Attach the other side length and then the top length in the same way. Fill all screw holes and apply a second coat of varnish to the visible lumber.

Finishing Touches

It is the details that make the difference, and these final projects will help to turn your yard into the ultimate retreat.

Yin-Yang Bird Table

The symbol of perfect balance is used in this colorful yet practical bird table that provides food and water for the wildlife and spreads good karma.

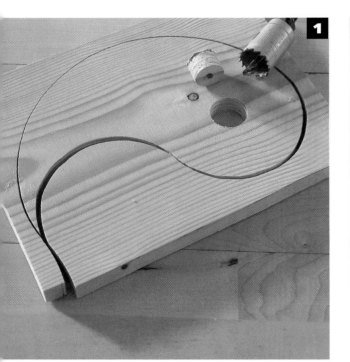

1 Enlarge the templates by 400 percent and transfer them onto the lumber (see *Template Techniques*, page 114). Using a jigsaw (see *Core Techniques*, page 108), cut out the shapes. Drill the smaller holes marked on the template with a 1¹/₄-in. hole saw (see *Further Techniques*, page 111).

2 Choose a bowl for the water dish. This can be any size—as long as it fits into the larger piece of the table—but it must have a rim. Measure the diameter of the bowl—not including the rim—and mark and cut a hole the right size with a hole saw or a jigsaw (see *Further Techniques*, page 110).

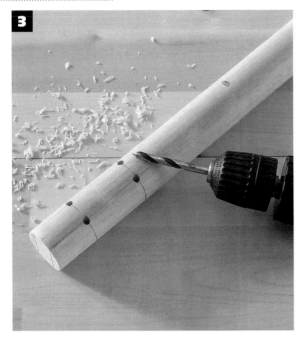

3 Measure and mark pencil lines around the long length of dowel, 1¹⁄₂ in. and 3¹⁄₄ in. from one end. Using a ¹⁄₄-in. drill bit (see *Core Techniques*, page 108), drill two parallel holes through the dowel, ³⁄₄ in. apart, on each marked line. When drilling through dowels, always clamp them firmly before you start, and drill carefully to avoid splitting the wood. Sand and then stain all the pieces of the bird table with exterior wood stain.

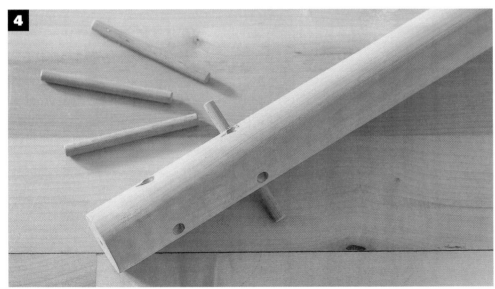

4 Push a short dowel peg through each of the lower holes in the long length of dowel.

5 Slide the 1¹⁄₄-in. hole in the larger piece of the bird table over the top of the dowel, and push it down to touch the pegs.

6 Push the remaining two pegs through the remaining holes in the long length of dowel, then slide the other piece of the table down onto the pegs. Adjust the two parts of the table so that when they are seen from above they make the yin-yang symbol.

7 Bird feeders are available from pet stores and most already have a hole in the bottom. If there isn't one, then drill a hole. Drill a $1/16$-in. pilot hole in the center of the top of the long piece of dowel. Take the top off the feeder, and drive a screw through the hole in the bottom into the pilot hole. Push the bird table into the ground, and fit the water dish in place.

Sundial

Sunflowers were the inspiration for this country garden sundial. If, however, your yard is full of roses or other flowers, change the color scheme to match.

YOU WILL NEED

Face

Plywood
- 1 piece: 3/8 x 15½ x 15½ in.
- 1 piece: 3/8 x 2¼ x 5½ in.

Birch ply
- 1 piece: 1/16 x 5½ x 6¾ in.

Stem

Birch ply
- 1 piece: 1/16 x 4 x 30 in.

Dowel
- 1 length: 1 x 31½ in.

- Face, pointer holder, pointer, and leaf templates on page 125
- Jigsaw
- Drill
- 3/16-in. drill bit and 1-in. spade bit
- Box cutter
- Ruler
- Pencil
- Emulsion paints
- 3/8-in.- and 1-in.-wide paintbrushes
- Fine artist's paintbrush
- Waterproof varnish

Screw
- 1: 1 5/8 in.

- Wood glue
- Staple gun
- 5/8-in. staples

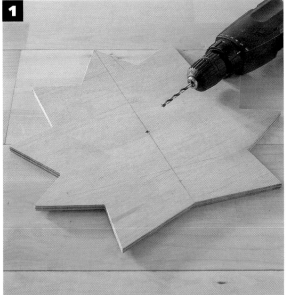

1 Enlarge the face template by 300 percent, and transfer it onto the square piece of plywood (see *Template Techniques*, page 114). Using a jigsaw (see *Core Techniques*, page 108), cut out the face. Predrill and countersink (see *Core Techniques*, page 109) a 3/16-in. hole in the center, as marked on the template.

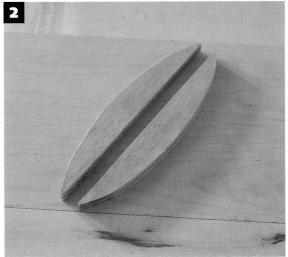

2 Cut down the face template to the shaded section to make the pointer holder template, and transfer it onto the small piece of plywood. Using a jigsaw, cut out the two identical shapes.

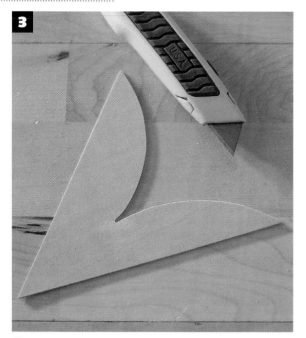

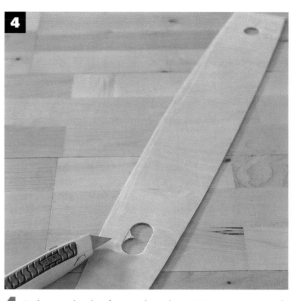

3 Enlarge the pointer template by 300 percent, and transfer it onto the face piece of birch plywood. Cut out the shape with a box cutter, scoring lightly and then more deeply until the plywood separates.

4 Enlarge the leaf template by 300 percent, and transfer it onto the stem piece of birch plywood. Cut out the shape with a box cutter, as before. Using a 1-in. spade bit (see *Further Techniques*, page 111), drill the three holes marked on the template. Draw a straight pencil line between the two touching holes, as shown, and using a box cutter, cut away the excess plywood on both sides to make an oval shape. Sand and then paint all the pieces (see below).

TIP

To achieve the sunflower effect, use a ⅜-in-wide paintbrush and paint the entire face of the sundial in lime-yellow emulsion. While this is still wet, drag a little lemon-yellow and egg-yellow emulsion through it. Start each brush stroke in the center and drag outwards. Brush over the face, following the original brush strokes, with a dry brush to blend the colors together. When the paint is dry, lay the template on the surface and make a pencil mark at each end of the time lines marked on the template. Lightly connect the marks to establish the time lines.

Using a fine artist's paintbrush, paint over each pencil line in egg-yellow emulsion, and leave to dry. Carefully paint a fine, dark-green line over each yellow line. Following the template, paint the Roman numerals onto the sundial. Using a ⅜-in-wide paintbrush, paint the leaf and stem with watered-down, dark-green emulsion, and wipe away any excess paint. While it is still wet, drag a little lime-yellow emulsion through it.

When all the paint is dry, seal it with two coats of waterproof varnish.

5

5 Drive a screw (see *Core Techniques*, page 109) down through the predrilled hole in the face into the top of the dowel.

6

6 Slide the oval hole in the leaf onto the dowel, then bend the leaf and slip the round hole onto the dowel. Slide the leaf a little way up the dowel.

7

7 Glue (see *Core Techniques*, page 109) the wider side of the pointer between the two halves of the pointer holder. The ends of the pointer should both protrude an equal amount.

8

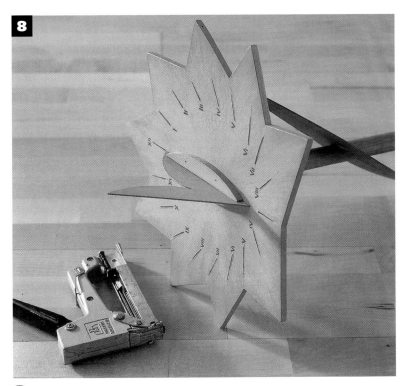

8 Staple (see *Further Techniques*, page 112) the pointer holder to the face of the sundial, with the lower end of the pointer $1^7/_8$ in. up from the bottom of the face.

Boot Scraper

An easy-to-make and practical project for all gardeners everywhere, this boot scraper has a metal scraper plate and boot brushes to keep the mud outside, where it belongs.

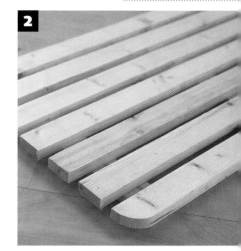

2 Predrill and countersink (see *Core Techniques*, page 109) seven $3/16$-in. holes in each of the three short lumber crosspieces. Position the holes centrally, with one 1¼ in. from each end and five spaced evenly between them.

Make up a slatted mat, with the curved slats on the outer edges. Lay the slats out, aligning the ends and using the ¾-in. spacers to separate them. Lay the short pieces across the slats with one 2¾ in. from each end and one positioned centrally between them. The predrilled holes should align with the center of each slat. Drive a 1¼-in. screw through each predrilled hole into a slat. On the second and sixth slats, drive in another screw, at an angle to the first one, to keep the mat from twisting. Sand the mat and then wax it with waterproof wood wax (see *Finishing Techniques*, page 114).

1 Mark a curve on one corner of each end of two of the long lumber slats. Using a jigsaw (see *Core Techniques*, page 108), cut out the curves.

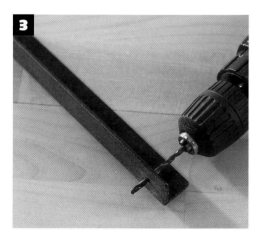

4 Choose one side and one end of the mat to work from for the next two steps. In the fourth slat, drill two $1/16$-in. holes. Position the holes centrally, with one 4 $3/8$ in. and one 13$3/8$ in. from the end. Drive $5/8$ in. screws through the holes in the angle iron into the holes in the slat.

3 Using a 1$3/4$-in. metal-cutting drill bit, drill two holes in one side of the angle iron. Position the holes centrally, with one $3/4$ in. from each end.

5 Turn the mat over. In the second and fifth slats, predrill and countersink two $3/16$-in. holes. Position the holes centrally, with one 3$5/8$ in. and one 14$1/4$ in. from the ends of the slats. Position the broom heads across the slats under the mat, spacing them evenly between the predrilled holes and aligning the ends. Drive 1$1/2$-in. screws through the predrilled holes into the broom heads.

Drink Tray

Nothing is more welcome than a cool drink on a hot summer day. The curved bottom of this tray is specially designed to create little "feet," so the tray will not tip on the grass and spill your drinks.

YOU WILL NEED

MDF
- 2 pieces: ⅜ x 6⅜ x 20¼ in.
- 2 pieces: ⅜ x 6⅜ x 12¼ in.

Quadrant
- 2 lengths: ½ x 8⅞ in.

Plywood
- 1 piece: ¹⁄₁₆ x 9½ x 14½ in.

- End and side templates on page 126
- Staple gun
- ⅝-in staples
- Jigsaw
- Drill
- ¹⁄₁₆-in. drill bit
- 1¼-in. hole saw

- Pencil
- Ruler
- Wood glue

Panel pins
- 8: ¾ in.

- Hammer
- Filler
- 120-grit sandpaper
- Sanding block
- Primer
- Satinwood paint
- Paintbrush

TIP

The paint will protect the tray from rain, but as it is made from MDF, it should not stay outdoors permanently.

1 Staple the two long pieces of MDF together (see *Further Techniques*, page 112). Enlarge the side template by 400 percent, and transfer it onto

the MDF (see *Template Techniques*, page 114), including the dashed lines, which should be transferred onto both pieces. Using a jigsaw (see *Core Techniques*, page 108), cut out the shapes, then predrill the $^1/_{16}$-in. holes, as marked. Pull out the staples to make two identical shapes.

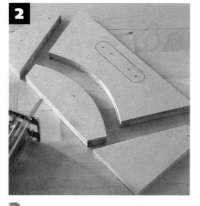

2 Staple the two short pieces of MDF together. Enlarge the end template by 400 percent, and transfer it onto the MDF. Using a jigsaw, cut out the shapes. Pull out the staples to make two identical shapes.

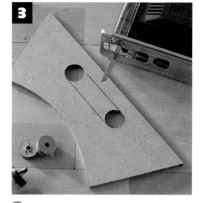

3 Using a 1¼-in. hole saw (see *Further Techniques*, page 111), drill the two holes, as marked. Draw straight pencil lines between them, and using a jigsaw, cut along the lines to make handle holes.

5 Run a thin line of glue (see *Core Techniques*, page 109) along the pencil line on one end of a side piece and

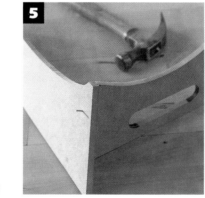

4 Staple a length of quadrant to each end piece, with one flat side ¾ in. below the handle holes.

butt an end piece up to it. Hammer panel pins through the predrilled holes in the sides into the edge of the end piece. Repeat the process with the other side and end pieces to make two L-shapes.

TIP

When hammering in panel pins, first hammer them through the predrilled holes so that the tips just protrude on the far side of the wood. Then, when you present the edge of the joining piece up to them, you can see exactly where the pins are.

6 Glue and pin the two L-shapes together in the same way, aligning the free edge of each end with the remaining pencil lines on the sides.

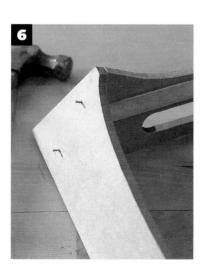

7 Run a line of glue along each length of quadrant, and fit the plywood base on top of them. When the glue is dry (approximately 30 minutes), fill the pin holes and sand the tray, then prime and paint it with two coats of satinwood paint (see *Finishing Techniques*, page 114).

Core
Techniques

These are the basic techniques that you will need to master to complete almost every project in this book. Practice them on scrap pieces of wood until you are confident of your ability.

1 Cutting with a crosscut saw

Because a crosscut saw is long and does not have strengthening along

the top, you have to take care that the blade does not flex while you are sawing—practice will pay off here.

2 Cutting with a backsaw

Draw the saw across the wood once or twice to create a small notch before you start cutting. The blade

will be more stable, and you will find it easier to cut accurately.

3 Cutting with a jigsaw

The key to accurate cutting is to make sure that the surface is firmly secured (in a workbench, for example)—and to take your time. Simply guide the blade along the line that you have drawn, and if you go off course for any reason, don't panic; stop and restart in the right

direction. Minor mistakes can be smoothed away with sandpaper. For the best results, the blade should always be sharp.

4 Drilling a hole

Mark the center of the hole that you want to drill with an X. Hold the drill perpendicular to the surface, so that you are not drilling at an angle. Start slowly, to move the bit into the center of the X and then put your weight behind it to drill through the wood.

5 Countersinking a screw

Do this on surfaces where it is important that screw holes are not visible. Predrill a hole (as in 4), then push the countersink bit into it to create a hole with sloped sides into which the screw fits, with its head

below the surface of the wood.

When countersinking side pieces for a project, take care to work on opposite faces of the wood to produce right- and left-hand pieces with the countersinking on the outer faces.

6 Screwing two pieces of wood together

Check that you have the correct size

of screw; it should be long enough to fit through the top layer and at least half the bottom layer of wood. In this book we have used 1/8-in.-thick countersink screws with crossheads, unless stated otherwise.

7 Nailing two pieces of wood together

Check that you have the right nails: too short and they will not be secure, too long and they will come through the other side of the wood. The nail should be hammered in straight.

8 Gluing, screwing, and clamping

Follow the instructions on the glue that you buy, as some will vary.

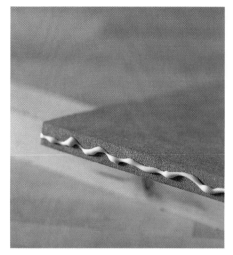

a) Apply glue to one or both of the sides to be joined (this may depend on the type of glue). Push and then screw the pieces of wood together.

b) If you are not screwing the two pieces together immediately, use clamps to firmly secure them while the glue dries. Using a damp cloth, wipe away any glue that has squeezed out from the joint, before it has a chance to harden.

Further Techniques

Many of the projects in this book require some of these techniques. As with the core techniques, if you have never attempted a particular technique before, practice it before embarking on the project you have chosen.

1 Cutting a straight line in a miter block

Miter blocks are an invaluable way of ensuring that a straight line is really straight. Simply lay the piece of wood

in the block, slot a backsaw through the parallel notches on either side, and saw down through the wood. Clamping a miter block in a workbench gives it extra stability and makes the work easier.

2 Cutting a miter in a miter block

Mitered edges are cut at 45° so they form neat corners when joined

together. Use the same principle as cutting straight lines, but this time, slot the blade of the saw through the two notches that are diagonally opposite one another.

3 Cutting out an internal circle

After drawing the circle—if you are right-handed—drill a hole inside its edge at the top right. Fit the blade of the jigsaw into the hole, and cut out the circle, cutting from right to left in a counterclockwise direction. If you are left-handed, drill the hole at the top left and cut clockwise.

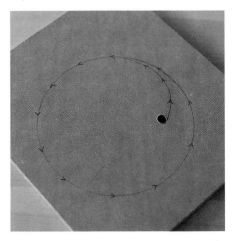

4 Using a bradawl

This tool ensures accuracy and is a good starting point, whether you are fixing screws or nails, or making a pilot hole for a fine drill bit. Find and

mark the exact center of the hole that you want to make with an X, then firmly dig in the pointed end of the bradawl into the center of the X.

5 Taping a drill bit

If you wish to drill into wood to a specified depth, rather than all the way through, simply measure along the bit from the point to your required depth, then wrap the area beyond with masking tape. Drill slowly,

and stop when the tape is flush with the surface of the wood, as you will have reached the correct depth.

6 Drilling with a spade bit

Mark the position of the hole with an X. Place the point of the spade bit exactly in the center of the X, and drill through the wood. For a neat finish, stop just as the point of the bit appears on the other side of the wood. Turn the wood over, place the

point of the bit in the hole and finish drilling from this side.

7 Drilling with a hole saw

Again, make an X, and place the long bit in the center of the hole saw exactly on it. Drill through the wood. You will find it easier to clamp the wood before you start, as the friction from the saw can cause it to spin around. For a neat finish, stop just as the long bit appears on the other side of the wood. Turn the wood over, place the point of the long bit in the hole, and finish drilling from this side. A hole saw will become blunt if it

gets too hot, so don't apply a lot of pressure when drilling—you will hear the drill slow down if you are pressing too hard—and back off intermittently to allow the cutter to cool down. Always remove the cutout piece of wood from the saw before cutting another hole.

8 Using a try square to mark parallel lines

The try square makes drawing parallel lines simple. Simply rest the top of the try square over the top edge of the piece that you are working on, at the marked point, and

draw a pencil line along the metal edge. Move the try square along by the required amount, and draw another line.

9 Clamping and protecting surfaces

Clamping is a very effective method of holding joints firmly while glue dries, but the clamp's hard, metal surfaces can damage the wood. To keep this from happening, simply slot

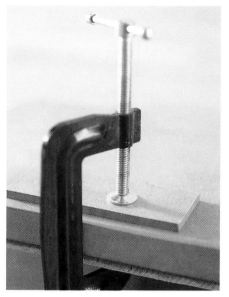

a thin offcut of wood or MDF between the surface and the jaws of the clamp.

10 Cutting thin dowels

With very narrow dowels, mark the area you want to cut, and hold a sharp box-cutter blade over the mark. Roll the dowel under the blade until it cuts in two. With slightly thicker dowels, use the same method to score the wood, then snap it in two and sand to finish.

11 Using a chisel and mallet

Clamp the wood or dowel you are going to chisel firmly in place before you start. Always chisel away from yourself. Do not be tempted to use a hammer instead of a mallet to drive the chisel; you will only damage the chisel's handle. Start by chiseling a deep line at the end point, so if the

wood splits while you are working, it should stop there. Do not try to cut out large pieces in one try; chisel off small sections from one side, at an angle, so that more is taken off the

top than the bottom, until you reach the end point. Turn the wood over and finish chiseling from the other side. If you are cutting a notch, try to choose a chisel that is exactly the right width for the neatest and easiest finish.

12 Stapling two pieces of wood together

Use this tool to fasten thin plywood or quadrant to thicker wood. Place the staple gun exactly where you want the staple to go, and squeeze the handle hard to fire the staple through the wood. If you are stapling plywood to a curved piece of wood,

as shown, space the staples approximately 2 in. apart, pushing the plywood down with one hand and firing the staples in with the other. We have used ⅝-in. staples throughout this book.

Finishing Techniques

A handmade project can be ruined by a poor finish. To give your work a professional look, spend time filling, sanding, and preparing the surfaces before you paint—it will make all the difference.

1 Filling a countersunk screw head

a) The countersunk screw head sits with its head a little below the surface of the wood.

b) Fill the countersink with car-body filler. We use this instead of traditional wood filler, which can contract as it dries, leaving you with a dent in the surface. Use a filler knife to smooth the filler into the countersink.

   If you are filling a deep hole, it is better to overfill and sand the bump back later. If you try to smooth it flat, you will find that the knife drags the filler out slightly.

c) When dry, simply sand the filler with 120-grit sandpaper. If you do this well, the original hole will be almost undetectable when painted.

2 Punching a nail

For a neat finish, use a nail punch to drive the head of the nail or pin down below the surface of the wood.

Hold the punch perpendicular to the nail and drive it down using a hammer. Fill the hole as you would for a countersunk screw head.

3 Filling and sanding an edge

a) The sawed edge of wood, particularly of plywood, is often rough. Use a filler knife to spread car-body

filler over the sawed edges. If you are filling a corner, as shown, make sure that the filler covers the joint as well.

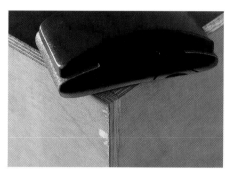

b) When the filler is dry, sand the edges with 120-grit sandpaper, and the filler will stay in the splinters and joints, giving a smooth surface.

4 Sealing an edge

If you are going to paint the wood

with water-based paint or varnish, then, once the edge is smooth, paint it with shellac sanding sealer first. This will keep the wood around the filler from absorbing water from the paint, which would cause it to swell slightly, leaving a depression or crack around the filled hole or joint.

5 Sanding a flat surface

A sanding block is the only way to remove dents and scratches from flat

surfaces. If you use sandpaper without a block, it tends to follow the depression, enlarging it rather than removing material from either side to flatten it. There are several types of blocks, although they all do basically the same job.

Sandpaper comes in different grades. In general, rough grades are used first, followed by finer ones to give a completely smooth finish. Wet-and-dry paper is used between coats of paint or varnish, almost

polishing the surface, making it completely smooth, and removing any trapped dust or flecks of wood and paint. Always finish with a coat of paint or varnish (unless you are distressing a surface), as the action of sanding will affect the finished color.

Keep the block parallel to the surface you are sanding, and on a large surface, move it in small circles to avoid making dents in the wood. We sand pieces smooth with 120-grit sandpaper if they are to be painted, but give them a final, additional rub down with 240-grit if they are going to be stained or just varnished.

6 Sanding a rounded edge

Use the same principle as before, but this time angle the sanding block so that it removes the edge of the

wood. This is easier if the wood is clamped in place.

7 Sanding a corner

Use the same principle to remove the corners of a piece of wood. Sharp

corners and edges will tend to chip and don't hold paint or varnish very well. It is also a good safety precaution to remove corners, especially on low-level items, such as benches.

8 Sanding the inside of a circle

Wrap a length of dowel or pencil in sandpaper to easily work it around the inside diameter of the cut circle. Use the same principle to sand the

insides of holes drilled with a spade bit or hole saw.

9 Painting and staining

Always choose a suitable paint for the surface and the treatment it is going to receive. For outdoor furniture, use waterproof paints or exterior stains where possible, and if you use emulsion, always seal it with at least two coats of waterproof varnish. Test the varnish on an offcut before painting the whole project, as some exterior varnishes have a very

brown tinge and will really affect some paint colors.

However, no matter how well you seal it, no softwood furniture is completely hardy. You should revarnish it each year, and store it indoors during the winter.

Template Techniques

Many of the projects in this book have templates. Enlarge them on a photocopier by the given percentages; the bigger templates will need to be enlarged onto several sheets of paper that must then be taped together. Cut out the templates with scissors.

1 Transferring a template onto wood

The easiest way to do this is to use spray paper glue (available from stationery and art supply stores) to

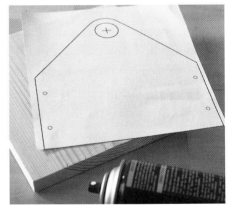

stick the cutout template onto the wood. However, you may find it clearer to draw around the template and remove it before cutting out the wood; this is what we have done throughout this book. If you do this, then you also have to transfer any marks on the template onto the wood. For screw holes, push a pencil through the X within the circle and mark the wood. Remove the template and draw an X over your mark. For larger shapes, cut them out of the template with scissors, lay the template on the wood, and draw around the shapes.

2 Cutting out shapes

Using a jigsaw, cut around the outer lines on the template, or around your drawn lines. On large pieces you may find it easier to cut out the shape roughly first, then go back and cut it

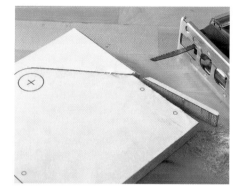

out neatly. Cut out curved shapes in sections; where this applies in a project, we have shown the cut-out piece surrounded by the offcuts to show you the best way to cut out the pieces.

3 Drilling holes marked on the template

Either drill through the paper and wood, placing the point of the bit on

the X within the circle, or mark the wood, as described in 1.

4 Screwing two pieces of wood together

This is a very useful technique when you want to cut two identical shapes. Lay the template on the wood first and note any marks. Use 1¼-in. screws to fasten the pieces of wood together, without screwing too close to the outline. Transfer the template

onto the wood, and cut out the shapes and drill any holes, as described in 2 and 3. Sand the edges if necessary, then unscrew the pieces of wood to give two identical shapes. Any screw holes can be filled when finishing the project.

If you prefer, you can stick the template onto one of the pieces of wood and then screw the two pieces together. If there are predrill holes marked on the template, drive the screws through those to avoid making unnecessary holes.

5 Using a router

This is an invaluable technique if you need to produce a number of identical shapes. A router is an expensive piece of equipment to buy, but they can be rented from tool-rental stores.

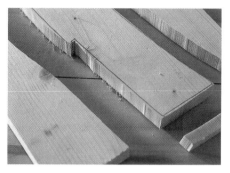

a) First cut out the template in thin MDF, using the technique described in 2, and sand the edges smooth. Place the template on the wood and draw around it in pencil. Using a jigsaw, cut out the shape roughly, cutting close to the pencil lines, but not within them.

b) Screw or pin the MDF template to the wood, positioning it exactly on the drawn lines. Using a router with a template profiling bit, rout around the template. This bit has a free-spinning wheel that runs along the MDF and a straight cutting edge below that cuts the wood to the same line as the template. Remove the template.

Toolbox

This is a good basic tool kit, though you don't need everything shown here for every project in this book. Before you begin a project, check to make sure that you have all the necessary tools; there's nothing more frustrating than having to stop halfway through a project because you don't have all the equipment.

Invest in a decent-sized toolbox in which to store everything. These boxes are inexpensive and can be found in a variety of sizes.

Finally, take care of your tools. If you keep them clean and free from dust, they will last longer and perform well.

Steel safety ruler

Box cutter

Retractable tape measure

Spirit level

Pencil

Scissors

Try square

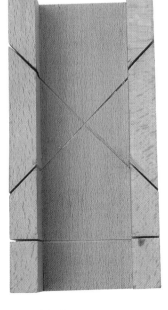

Miter block

Backsaw

Jigsaw

Crosscut saw

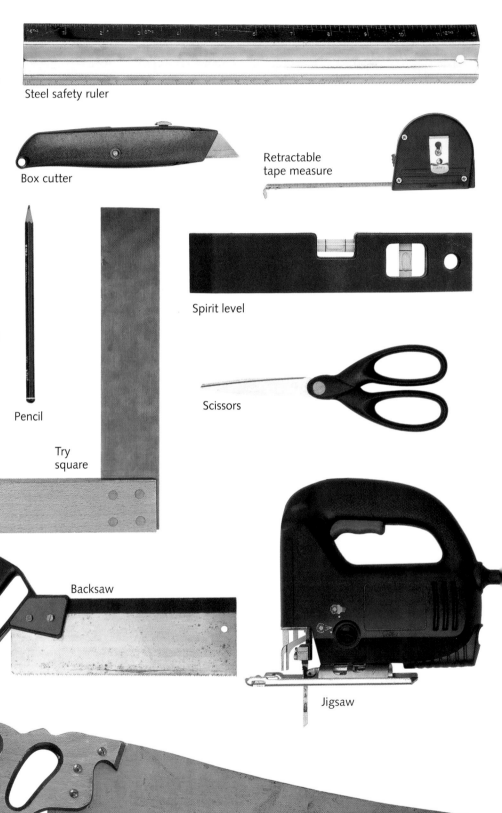

Countersink bit

Power drill

Hole saw

Spade bit

Straight bit

Chisel

Pin hammer

Claw hammer

Staple gun

Selection of nails and screws

Corner clamp

C-clamp

Wood adhesive

Filler knife

Car-body filler

Sandpaper in several grades, including wet and dry, with sanding block

Pliers

Flathead screwdriver

Crosshead screwdriver

Bradawl

Nail center punch

Flat paintbrush

Artist's brush

Templates

The percentages given beside each template indicate the percentage by which it must be enlarged to make it the correct size. Measurements are also given to help you check that your enlarged template is the correct size. It is important to double-check these measurements on your enlarged template, as not all photocopiers enlarge completely accurately. The shaded areas denote subtemplates within the full template or areas to be cut away. These are also specified in the project text.

The marks on the templates follow the following legend:

(+) Holes to be drilled or predrilled

- - - - - - - - Marks to be transferred

▦ Areas to be cut away or cut out to form another template

·············· Alignment guides

——   —— Center lines for guidance only

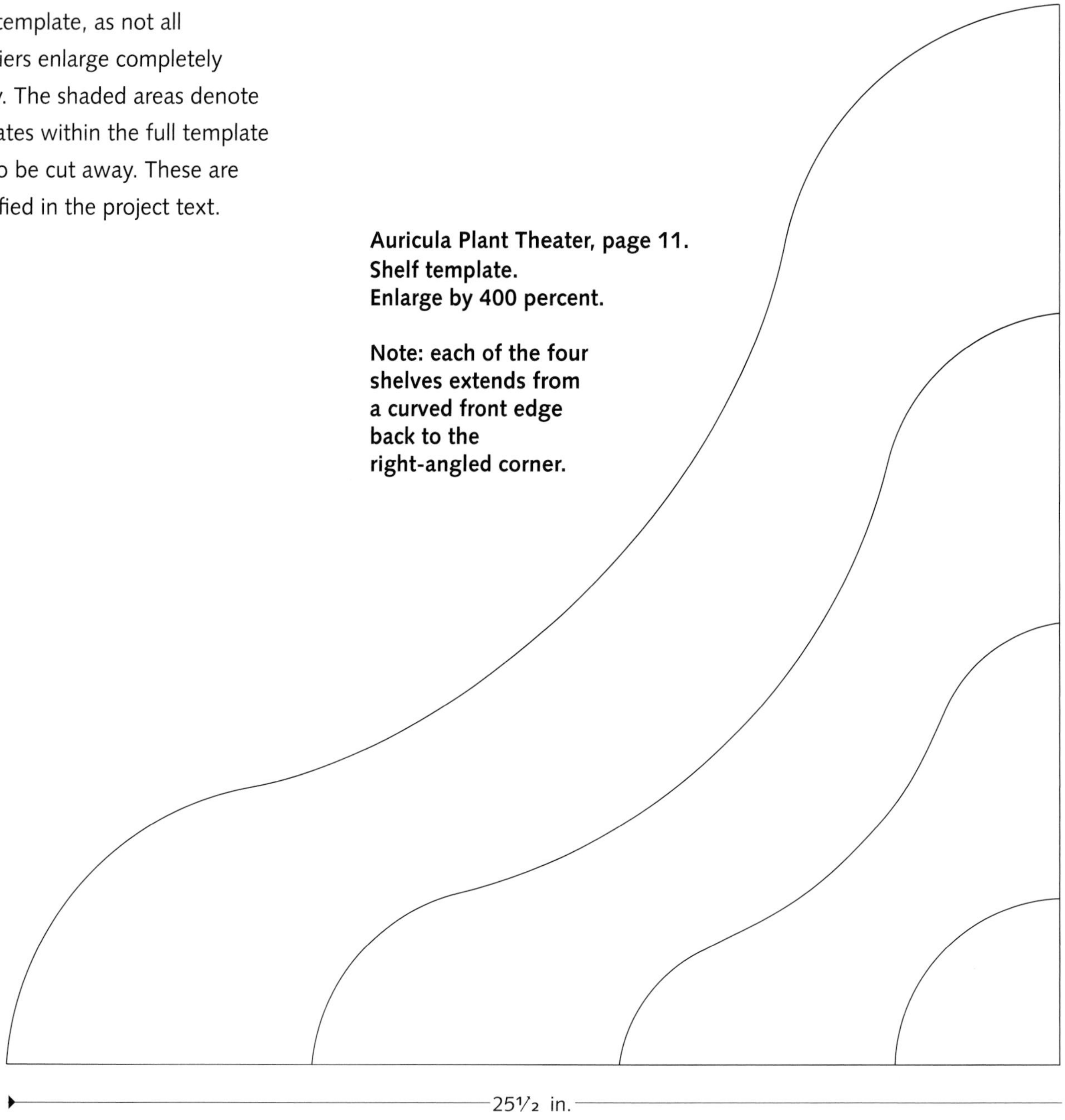

**Auricula Plant Theater, page 11.
Shelf template.
Enlarge by 400 percent.**

**Note: each of the four
shelves extends from
a curved front edge
back to the
right-angled corner.**

25½ in.

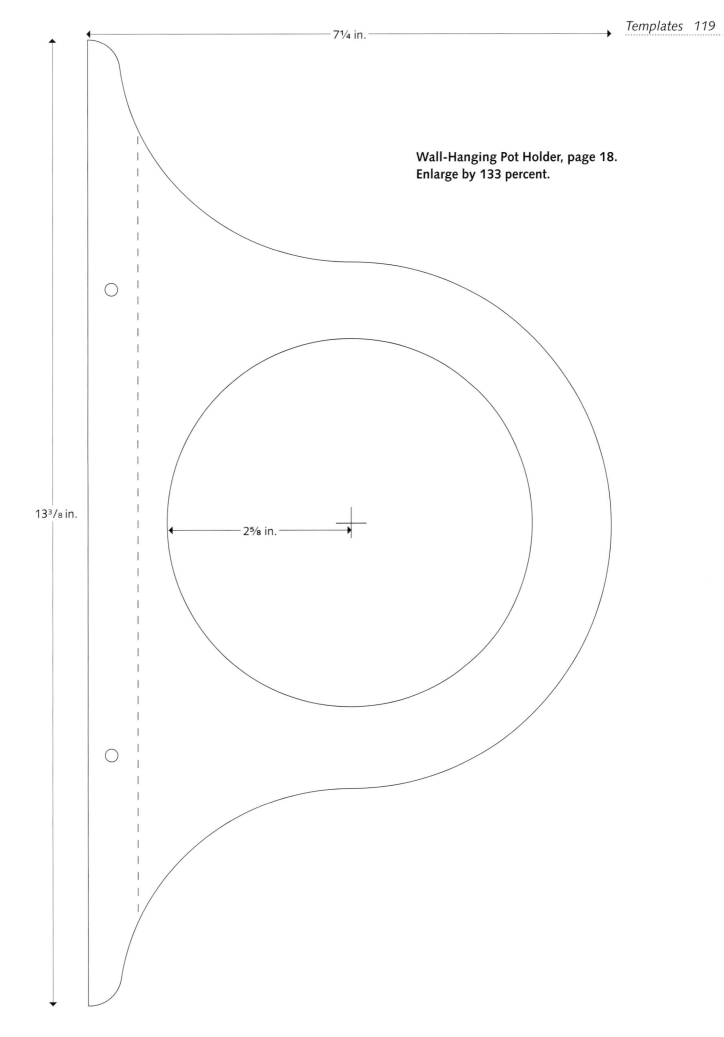

7¼ in.

13³/₈ in.

2⁵/₈ in.

**Wall-Hanging Pot Holder, page 18.
Enlarge by 133 percent.**

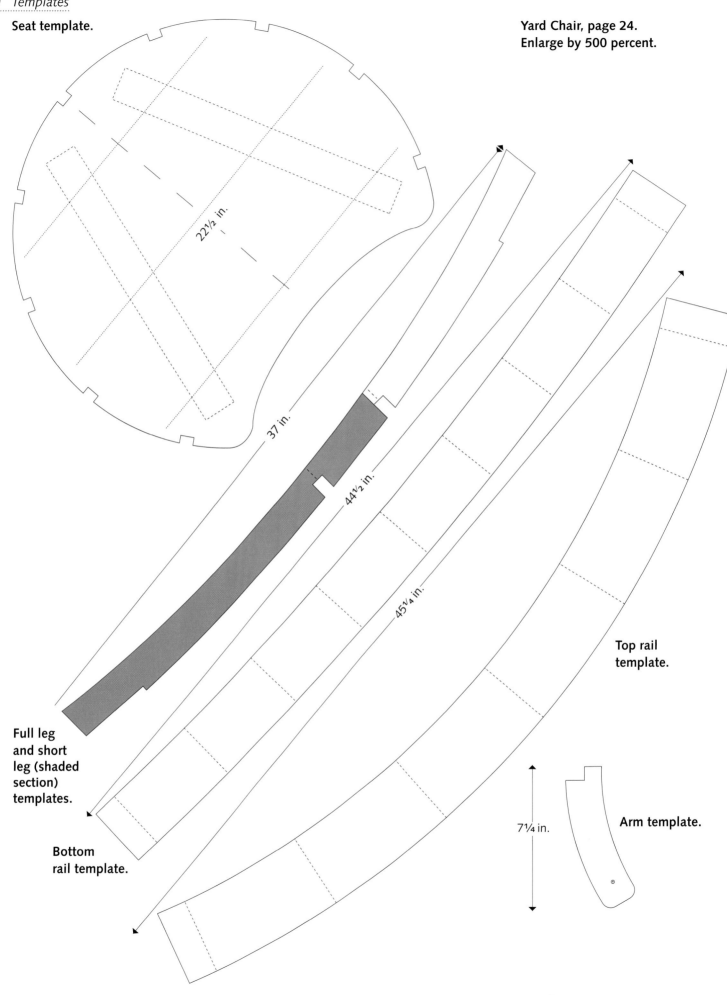

Seat template.

**Yard Chair, page 24.
Enlarge by 500 percent.**

22½ in.

37 in.

44½ in.

45¼ in.

**Full leg
and short
leg (shaded
section)
templates.**

**Bottom
rail template.**

**Top rail
template.**

7¼ in.

Arm template.

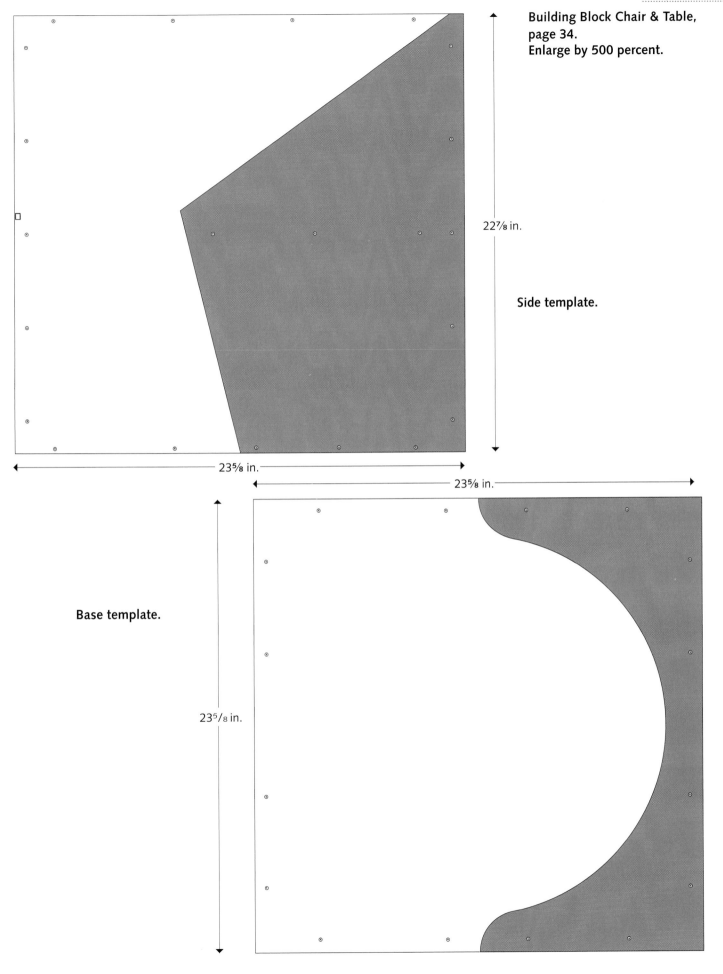

**Building Block Chair & Table,
page 34.
Enlarge by 500 percent.**

22⁷⁄₈ in.

Side template.

23⁵⁄₈ in.

23⁵⁄₈ in.

Base template.

23⁵⁄₈ in.

Barbecue Table, page 40. Side and container partition (shaded section) templates. Enlarge by 665 percent.

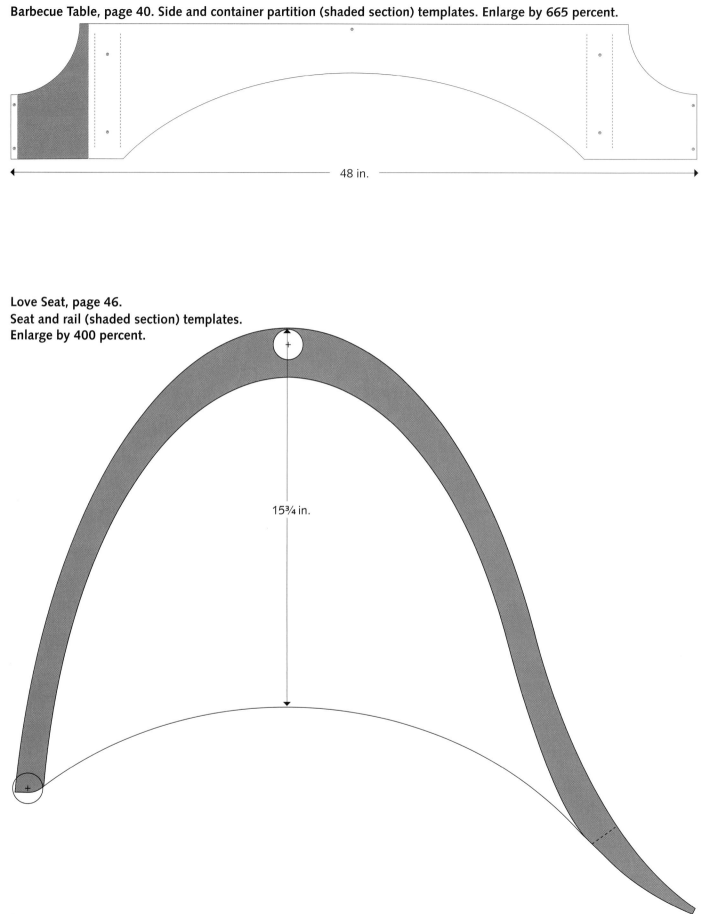

← 48 in. →

Love Seat, page 46.
Seat and rail (shaded section) templates.
Enlarge by 400 percent.

15¾ in.

← 28⅜ in. →

Tool Rack, page 55. Enlarge by 400 percent.

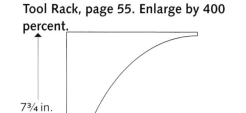

7¾ in.

Tool Caddy, page 58. Enlarge by 400 percent.

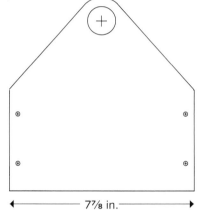

7⅞ in.

Potting Bench, page 67. Leg top template. Enlarge by 400 percent.

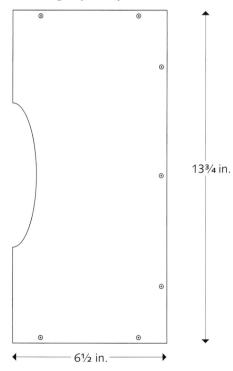

13¾ in.

6½ in.

Potting Bench, page 67. End leg and side leg (shaded section) templates. Enlarge by 400 percent.

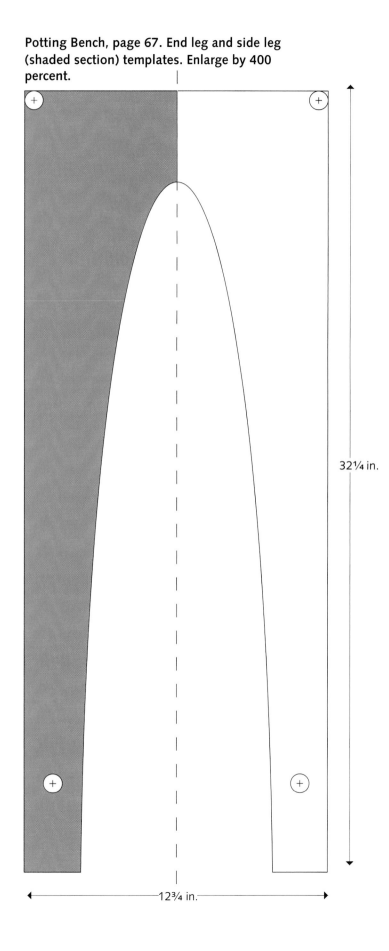

32¼ in.

12¾ in.

Seat for a Child's Swing, page 82.
Seat and rail (shaded section) templates.
Enlarge by 400 percent.

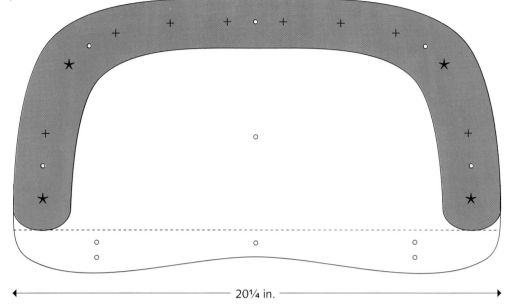

20¼ in.

Japanese Arbor, page 86.
Enlarge by 665 percent.

End beam template.

4 in.

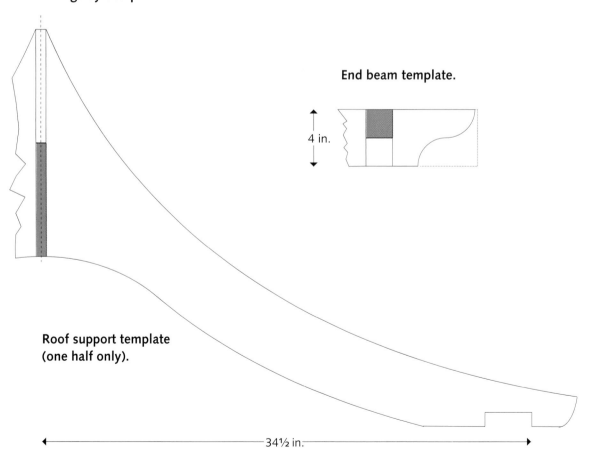

Roof support template
(one half only).

34½ in.

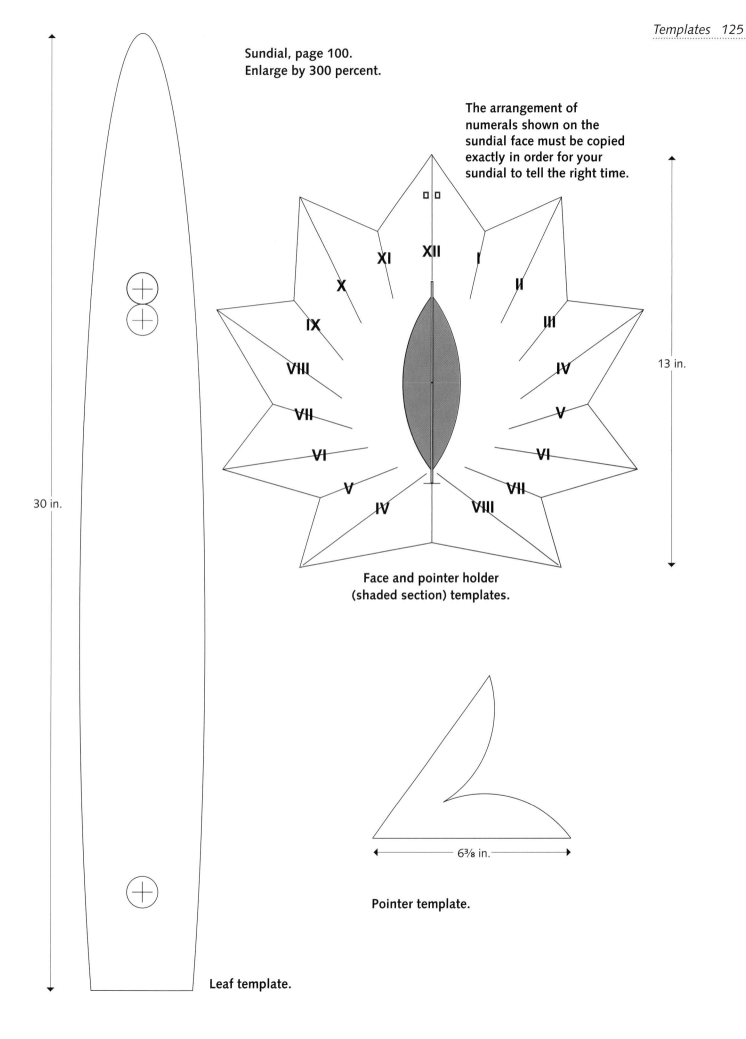

Sundial, page 100.
Enlarge by 300 percent.

The arrangement of
numerals shown on the
sundial face must be copied
exactly in order for your
sundial to tell the right time.

13 in.

30 in.

Face and pointer holder
(shaded section) templates.

6⅜ in.

Pointer template.

Leaf template.

Yin-Yang Bird Table, page 96.
Enlarge by 400 percent.

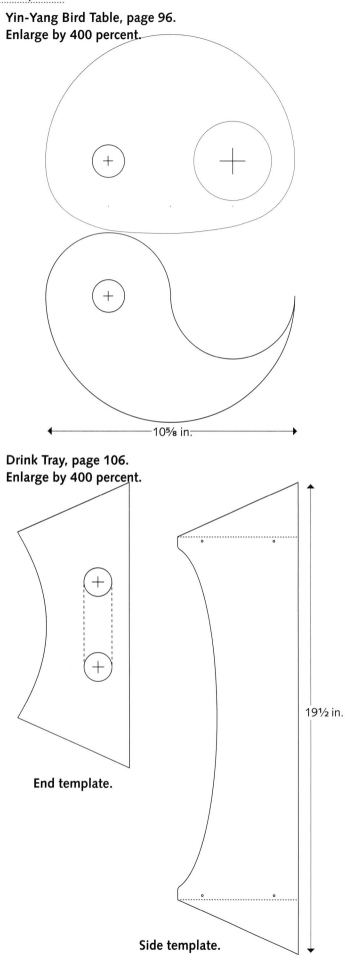

10⅝ in.

Drink Tray, page 106.
Enlarge by 400 percent.

End template.

19½ in.

Side template.

Materials

Birch plywood

This is a thin, very flexible board made from several layers of birch wood bonded together. It is perfect for making curves.

Take care when cutting birch plywood, as most pieces will bend more along the length of the board than across the width. For the projects in this book it is essential that the maximum bend is along the length of the cut shape.

MDF

MDF (medium-density fiberboard) is easy to work with and is relatively inexpensive. Its smooth surface is perfect for paint finishes, but it is not waterproof. The dust from cutting MDF can be irritating, so always wear a mask and work in a well-ventilated area.

Lumber

The lumber used throughout this book is pine, which is readily available from home improvement stores. Choose lumber carefully; avoid pieces that are bowed or split, like the piece shown here. To check if

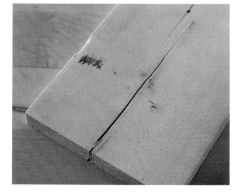

a piece is bowed, lay it on a flat floor and turn it over onto each side in turn. Any bowing should be easy to see, as the wood will not lie flat on the floor.

Try to buy well-seasoned wood, though this can be more expensive and not so readily available.

Marine plywood

A strong and rigid board made up from layers of wood bonded together with the layers running at right angles to one another and with waterproof glue. Better-quality boards are made up from more and thinner layers of wood, making them more stable.

We have used this material extensively throughout this book as it does not break down in wet conditions. However, it does have a tendency to fray on cut edges, and so it does need filling, sanding, and painting to look its best.

Suppliers

All the tools and materials used in this book can be bought from home improvement stores or lumber merchants. Consult your local telephone directory for outlets near you.

Glossary

Batten A strip of wood, often used to describe wood attached to a wall for holding a component in place.

Bevel Any angle, other than a right angle, cut on a piece of wood or found on a tool blade; to cut such an angle.

Chamfer A small 45-degree bevel planed along the edge of a piece of wood to make it less sharp; to plane such a bevel.

Countersink To drill a hole into wood to allow the entire head of a screw or bolt to end up below the surface.

Cross grain Grain that does not follow the main grain direction.

Dowel A short, round length of wood that is fitted into holes in two pieces of wood to hold them together; to fit such a piece of wood.

Dressed all round (DAR) A length of wood or plank that has had all four sides planed before being sold. The dimensions given, however, are for the wood before it was planed, so a DAR length will be smaller than these.

Dressed two sides (D2S) A length of wood or plank that has had two opposing sides planed.

Dry assembling Fitting together or assembling workpieces without fixing or gluing them, to check for an accurate fit and that all angles are true before final fixing.

End grain The irregular surface of wood that is exposed after cutting across the fibers.

Galvanized Screws or nails covered with a protective layer of zinc, used to prevent rusting in outdoor projects.

Grain The direction or alignment of the fibers in a piece of wood.

Groove A narrow channel cut along a piece of wood in the direction of the grain; to cut such a channel.

Hardwood Wood that comes from deciduous, broad-leafed trees—not necessarily harder than softwood.

Jig A device, often homemade, for holding a piece of work in position and enabling repeated working to be done.

Laminate A flat surface made by bonding different layers together, such as plastic, melamine, etc.; to make such a board.

Marine or waterproof plywood A plywood made with water-resistant hardwood layers and strong glue, used for exterior projects and those where moisture and condensation may occur.

Medium-density fiberboard (MDF) A versatile, smooth-surfaced man-made board, produced by binding wood dust together with glue.

Miter A corner joint for which two pieces of wood are cut with bevels of equal angles, usually 45 degrees; to cut such a joint.

Molding A length of wood, either hardwood or softwood, that has a shaped profile.

Offcut A piece of scrap wood left over after a workpiece has been cut.

Pilot hole A small hole drilled into wood that acts as a guide for the thread of a wood screw.

Plywood A strong man-made board produced by gluing thin layers of board together—often faced with hardwood or softwood veneer.

Primer The first coat of paint on bare wood, designed to seal the surface and provide a base for subsequent coats.

Rabbet A recess, step, or groove, usually rectangular, that is cut into a piece of wood to allow a mating piece to be inserted there.

Slat A narrow, usually thin, length of wood used as part of an identical series to form a fence, chair seat, etc.

Softwood Wood that comes from coniferous trees—this is not necessarily softer than hardwood.

Template A pattern or shape, usually drawn on cardboard, paper, or thin board, used as a guide for accurate marking on wood or man-made boards, especially when more than one identical piece is required.

Tongue-and-groove A joint in which a thin tongue of wood on one piece of wood is fitted into a matching groove on another—mainly used in doors and wall panels.

True Describes when something is exact; e.g., a true right angle is perfectly accurate; to smooth perfectly flat with a plane, chisel, or sander.

With the grain Working wood along the direction or alignment of the fibers.

Workpiece A piece of wood or project that is unfinished and still being worked on.

Acknowledgments

Philip and Kate would like to thank John Symons, Jane McCallum, Jules and Andy Knight, John Samuels, John Wells, and Alan, Carol, and Andrea Winslade for generously allowing us to photograph in their gardens and for their unswerving hospitality in the face of a horde.

A special thanks to Lucinda Symons for her fantastic photography, which brings out the best in us and our work; Holly Jolliffe for sterling assisting and constant good humor; Denise Brock for her impeccable styling; and Roger Daniels for making these pages look so good.

Enormous thanks to Andy Knight for space, access to materials, and time off, without which we couldn't have done this book. Thanks also to his crew for helpful suggestions and lots of encouragement.

Thanks a lot to Cindy Richards and Georgina Harris for commissioning us in the first place and for their continued support.

Thanks also to Steve Gott and Denise Brock for designing and making the projects on pages 16, 20, and 81.

Thanks to Roger Oates Design (tel: 00 44 1531-632718) for lending the Fagotin Chestnut chair and table seen with the *Willow Screen* on page 92.